BLACKSTONE'S GUIDE

The Bribery Act 2

CW00959671

BLACKSTONE'S GUIDE TO

The Bribery Act 2010

Monty Raphael
Special Counsel, Peters & Peters

Contributing authors
Neil Swift, Partner, Peters & Peters
and Rachna Gokani, Barrister,
QEB Hollis Whiteman

OXFORD
UNIVERSITY PRESS

OXFORD

UNIVERSITY PRESS

Great Clarendon Street, Oxford OX2 6DP

Oxford University Press is a department of the University of Oxford.
It furthers the University's objective of excellence in research, scholarship,
and education by publishing worldwide in

Oxford New York

Auckland Cape Town Dar es Salaam Hong Kong Karachi
Kuala Lumpur Madrid Melbourne Mexico City Nairobi
New Delhi Shanghai Taipei Toronto

With offices in

Argentina Austria Brazil Chile Czech Republic France Greece
Guatemala Hungary Italy Japan Poland Portugal Singapore
South Korea Switzerland Thailand Turkey Ukraine Vietnam

Oxford is a registered trade mark of Oxford University Press
in the UK and in certain other countries

Published in the United States
by Oxford University Press Inc., New York

First published 2010

British Library Cataloguing in Publication Data

Data available

Library of Congress Cataloging in Publication Data

Data available

Typeset by Cepha Imaging Private Ltd, Bangalore, India
Printed in Great Britain
on acid-free paper by
CPI Antony Rowe

ISBN 978-0-19-957978-5

3 5 7 9 10 8 6 4 2

Foreword

It was an immense relief for those who are concerned about this country's reputation for probity that in the dying days of the last Labour Government the Bribery Act became law. It had been long awaited. It had been preceded by two reports by the Law Commission and consultation exercises, but not withstanding the criticisms of the Organisation for Economic Co-operation and Development (OECD) as to the then law of the United Kingdom, it was only late in the day that the Bribery Act reached the statute book and even now, as I write this foreword, we still await the new government bringing the Act into force.

When the Act comes into force it will substantially improve our law and should have beneficial effects around the globe. It should encourage other countries—who, like the United Kingdom in the past, have neglected the need for having powers which enable action to be taken to deter corruption in general and bribery in particular—to adopt similar legislation. The problem with bribery is that once it becomes an embedded part of the culture of any country it undermines almost every aspect of the society of that country. It can undermine the courts and the rule of law. It can paralyse the government and undermine trade and commerce. A culture in which bribery is rampant is a particularly insidious problem for undeveloped or less developed countries who find that it almost inevitably attacks their institutions so that they are no longer able to protect their citizens. In addition it deters multinational companies from trading with a country in which bribery is prevalent. Global companies are increasingly concerned about their reputation and reluctant to expose themselves to allegations that they are contravening best international standards of propriety.

If it were ever the situation that a responsible company could justify falling below international standards on the basis that it is only 'doing in Rome what the Romans do', this is no longer the case. This is underlined by the international conventions to which this country has adhered. I have in mind the UN Convention against Corruption of October 2003 and the OECD Convention on Combating Bribery of Foreign Public Officials in International Business Transactions which came into force on 15 February 1999. The OECD Convention places an obligation on the signatory nations to establish a criminal offence under their law that makes it an offence for any person to intentionally offer, promise, or give any undue pecuniary or other advantage to a foreign public official.

It was a decade later that the Bribery Act was passed to fulfil that obligation and this, I believe, the Act succeeds in doing, as this excellent and timely book makes clear. Though the Bribery Act is almost exclusively dealing with the criminal law,

I suspect it will also have a significant influence on civil law, for example as to the obligations of directors to take appropriate action to prevent bribery, and indeed as to what constitutes bribery. The Act is also unusual for criminal legislation in that it is extra-territorial in effect; it applies to conduct occurring outside what is normally the jurisdiction of this country; and it reverses the burden of proof (which usually constitutes a contravention of Article 6 of the European Human Rights Convention, though here this is justifiable because the facts are usually peculiarly within the knowledge of proposed defendants). Offences under the Act will also create novel difficulties for those having to sentence. Although bribery offences can do great harm by undermining the culture of a country, they are examples of white collar crime which can require a different approach to determining the appropriate sentence when the court is considering imposing a monetary penalty.

These are among the features of the Act that make this book extremely timely. It will provide very considerable assistance to those persons who could be affected by its provisions. This is especially true of those who trade with countries where bribery at present is much more common than it is in this country. They will be grateful for the clarity of the explanations given as to the meaning of the provisions of the Act, including the unusual features to which I have already referred. The many commercial concerns based in this country that trade internationally will appreciate the holistic approach adopted by the author. The fact that the explanations are given in their historical context will make them more easily understood. Judges and lawyers will also be greatly assisted as bribery is a growth area of the law which in the future is going to involve increasing amounts of the courts' and lawyers' (and their clients') time. As the editors correctly state:

It seems inevitable that in the first years of the working of this new legislation, those charged with superintending corporate compliance and ethical behaviour generally may have to have recourse to legal opinion until this legislation becomes more 'user friendly' through regular use and judicial pronouncements.

The publishers had better be prepared to respond to the inevitable demands for successive editions of this valuable work. In the meantime I warmly congratulate the author on producing an excellent first edition.

Lord Woolf
June 2010

Preface

The Bribery Act 2010 is fairly short for a radical measure designed to reform the law after a century marked by inactivity and inefficiency in tackling grand and petty corruption. Yet, such was its importance that all parties coalesced to bring the measure to a conclusion in the last hours of the last Parliament.

This Guide can do no more than explain what went before, what was lacking, and what drew widespread criticism of the old law's inadequacies. It seeks to understand Parliament's intentions and to prophesy the effect on future corporate behaviour.

Much is left to the courage of business to embrace the aims of the Act, and to be fairly and ethically competitive in the pursuit of shareholder value and the maintenance of communal morality.

The Act assumes, and relies heavily upon, the fairness and proportionality of prosecutors as it also does upon the wisdom of both judges and juries. It will be for them to justify the confidence that those regulated by this measure will not be oppressed by behavioural requirements that are unreasonable or disproportionate to the size and nature of the enterprise in question.

Any possible further editions will be better placed to address the Act's success or otherwise.

For the present, my collaborators and I are indebted to Oxford University Press for its invitation to us to bring this work on and we are particularly grateful for the patience and indulgences of our Assistant Commissioning Editor, Faye Judges.

Lord Woolf has flattered us by agreeing to provide the foreword and we thank him for setting aside the time to do so.

I must express my personal and sincere gratitude to my colleagues, Neil Swift and Rachna Gokani. The latter added the burdens of research and writing to her already busy life at the criminal bar. The shortcomings manifest in this work are attributable to me alone.

Lastly, my long-suffering family have remained uncomplaining and supportive as ever. Without the encouragement and help of all I have named, this Blackstone Guide would have remained a permanent work in progress.

Monty Raphael
June 2010

Contents—Summary

Contents—Detailed

Table of Cases

Table of Legislation

List of Abbreviations

BIS	Department for Business, Innovation and Skills
CIOB	Chartered Institute of Building
CJA 2003	Criminal Justice Act 2003
CPS	Crown Prosecution Service
CRO	civil recovery order
DOJ	Department of Justice
DPP	Director of Public Prosecutions
EAW	European arrest warrant
ECHR	European Convention on Human Rights
FCPA	(US) Foreign and Corrupt Practices Act 1977
FSA	Financial Services Authority
GMC	Multidisciplinary Group on Corruption
GRECO	The Group of States against Corruption
MLA	mutual legal assistance
OECD	Organisation for Economic Co-operation and Development
OECD Convention	OECD Convention on Combating Bribery of Foreign Public Officials in International Business Transactions
OFAC	Office of Foreign Assets Control
PEP	politically exposed person
POCA	Proceeds of Crime Act 2002
RCPO	Revenue and Customs Prosecution Office
SAR	suspicious activity report
SCA	Serious Crime Act 2007
SCPO	serious crime prevention order
SEC	Securities and Exchange Commission
SFO	Serious Fraud Office
SOCA	Serious Organised Crime Agency
SOCPA	Serious Organised Crime and Police Act 2005
TI	Transparency International
UNCAC	UN Convention Against Corruption
UNDP	United Nations Development Programme
USC	United States Code

1

INTRODUCTION

Like its predecessors in the series, this Blackstone's Guide is intended to introduce   1.01
the reader to a new piece of legislation and its likely effects. Because the Bribery Act
2010 is a root and branch reworking of the law of public and private corruption, its
clear intentions can be stated but its consequences only speculated upon. There are
some areas where some uncertainty is bound to persist and others which the Act
does not directly address at all.

What the Act does—and does simply and economically—is set out four new   1.02
bribery offences, which can be committed by corporations and individuals. The Act
assumes a wide territorial jurisdiction. It also assumes a willingness by business to
protect itself by objectively judged 'adequate procedures'. In addition, the Act
emphasizes the gravity with which bribery is regarded by imposing very severe
sanctions.

Uncertainty still attends how prosecutorial discretion will be exercised, particu-   1.03
larly in the cases of facilitation payments, corporate hospitality, promotional expenditure, and corporate relationships in and with joint ventures, foreign subsidiaries,
and local agents. Guidance to be published in accordance with section 9 of the Act
will doubtless touch upon all of these issues, albeit generically. What will not be
available is an advice service such as that provided by the Department of Justice of
the United States in advance of embarking upon business transactions.

The best guide to Parliament's thinking on this bipartisan measure is as always,   1.04
Hansard. From there it is clear that while the elements of the offences are defined,
business is expected to adopt a risk-based approach and, indeed, a conservative risk-
based approach. Some further assistance may be derived from the Explanatory
Notes, prepared by the Ministry of Justice in order to assist an understanding of the
Act. They have not been considered by Parliament and thus their evidential value or
persuasive value is limited.

The Act is not retrospective; as such it is likely that a working knowledge of the   1.05
old law will be required for years to come, with many cases emerging in the future
that straddle both the old and the new regime.

Unlike some published guidance under the anti-money laundering regime, adher-   1.06
ence to guidance published under section 9 will not by itself provide a legal defence.
Rather, section 9 guidance is to be both the subject of further consultation with

business and a broad template to assist business to ready itself for the obligations imposed, particularly by sections 6 and 7 of the Act.

1.07   What the Act does not attempt to do, at least directly, is involve itself in such areas as trading in influence, the financing of political parties, the bribery of legislators (except when they can be defined as foreign public officials under section 6(5) or can be brought within the general bribery offences), cash-for-questions, and cash-for-honours. That is not to say that, save where Parliament legislates otherwise, or its privilege is invoked, courts will not interpret the Act widely as a general code, punishing all activities that may be brought within sections 1 and 2—the general bribery offences.

1.08   All the old law, both common law and statute, is replaced by this legislation. It no longer relies upon outmoded concepts, like those of master and servant, which dictated the framing of the Prevention of Corruption Act 1906. It attempts to spell out clearly what is meant by 'bribing' or 'being bribed' and side-steps troublesome issues such as dishonesty, which the common law appeared to manage very well without. Similarly, the words 'corruptly' or 'with intention to corrupt' do not appear in the statute.

1.09   The general bribery offences are split between section 1 (offering a bribe) and section 2 (receiving a bribe). Basically, the Act criminalizes the offer, promise, or gift of a financial or other advantage intending to influence a person to perform a relevant function improperly or to reward a person for the improper performance of a relevant function. It also criminalizes the same conduct on the part of the payer (P) if P believes that the acceptance of the advantage would by itself constitute the improper performance of a relevant function. In both cases it is immaterial whether the person to whom P offers, promises, or gives the advantage is the same person as the person who is to improperly perform the function. Similarly, it does not matter whether the advantage is offered, promised, or given by P or through a third party. Presumably, the number of third parties who may be involved is irrelevant.

1.10   Section 2 deals with the receipt of the bribe. It is an offence for the receiver (R) to request, agree to receive, or accept an advantage intending that in consequence R or another will improperly perform a relevant function. This covers the situation in which the request for a bribe, the agreement to accept a bribe, or acceptance itself constitutes improper performance of a relevant function without more. Also criminalized is a reward for the improper performance of a relevant activity, or an improper performance in anticipation of being bribed. Again the Act covers conduct where third parties are involved, ie in accepting the bribe or benefiting from it, or in being the actor who improperly performs the relevant function. Section 2 sets out four different scenarios legislating criminal conduct. In most of the scenarios it is not relevant whether R knew or believed that the performance of the function is or would be improper. Thus, the Act sets out to actively discourage anyone who is expected to act in good faith and impartially from even contemplating receiving any advantage for themselves or others. Any defence relying on subjectivity has been completely removed. This is one of the many areas where the Act is designed to make the task of the prosecutor easier by lightening the compass and burden of proof.

Sections 3 to 5 define the nature of the relevant function, what is meant by   1.11
improper performance, and the test to be applied in judging what level of proper
performance can be expected. The test laid down by the Act is that of the UK
reasonable person. Here, as in other parts of the Act, no concessions are made to
foreign local custom and practice.

Because the offences under sections 1 and 2 can be committed anywhere, as   1.12
defined by section 12, it is important to note that where a function is being performed that is not subject to the UK law, local custom and practice are to be ignored
unless permitted or required by the local written law. Thus, the former practice of
relying only on the opinion of local counsel, however distinguished in the country
in question, is no longer to be considered adequate.

Section 6 of the Act introduces for the first time the discrete offence of bribery of   1.13
a foreign public official. In so doing it meets one of the main criticisms of UK non-
compliance by the Bribery Working Group of the Organisation for Economic
Co-operation and Development (OECD). For this offence to be committed, P must
intend to influence the official in his capacity as a foreign public official with intent
to obtain or retain business or business advantage. Again, it is irrelevant whether the
bribe is paid directly or through a third party. As with section 5(2), whether or not
a foreign public official is permitted or required to be influenced by the offer, promise, or gift of an advantage is to be judged solely by any published written law applicable to that official. A foreign public official is defined by section 6(5) and extends
to legislators, administrators, and holders of judicial office and even to officials and
agents of public international organizations. This latter provision is doubtless aimed
at confronting the problem of the diversion of overseas aid to developing countries
or possibly the discouragement of the breach of international sanctions such as
occurred in connection with the Iraq oil-for-food programme. In that case, the UN's
own administrative office came under severe scrutiny.

Section 6 makes it clear that if it is contended that the official's functions were   1.14
permitted by written law, then, if those functions were to be performed in the United
Kingdom, the written law is that of the United Kingdom. Where the functions were
to be performed elsewhere, the written published law is that of the relevant state.
Where the official belongs to an international organization, then whether or not the
activity is permitted or required is to be judged by the written rules of that
organization.

For the purpose of section 6, 'business' is defined widely to include both trade and   1.15
professions.

Perhaps the most controversial new provision is section 7, which makes it an   1.16
offence for a commercial organization to fail to prevent bribery. The organization is
guilty of the offence if an employee or other person associated with it bribes another
with the intention of obtaining or retaining business or a business advantage for the
organization. The prosecution will need to prove that bribery did occur, but not that
it was prosecuted to conviction, or at all. The burden will then shift to the organization to prove that it had in place adequate procedures designed to prevent employees
or others associated with it from indulging in such conduct.

1.17 Clearly, organizations are henceforth required to assess the risk arising from the nature of their business, their counter parties, their subsidiaries, and their agents.

1.18 The Act covers not only UK incorporated companies and UK nationals, but also foreign companies carrying on business in the United Kingdom. It covers business within and outside the United Kingdom.

1.19 Who is to be deemed an associated person for the purposes of section 7 is explicitly defined by section 8 of the Act. Here, as elsewhere in the Act, emphasis is placed on the requirement that business pays more than merely lip-service in compliance with the Act's provisions, and this is reinforced by the clear requirement that prosecutors will not be limited by the written descriptions of relationships but will have regard in every case to all the relevant circumstances. One of the many abuses targeted by the draftsman of the Act is the use of consultants who provide fictitious or cosmetic services as a cover for receiving monies that can then be passed on to the appropriate public official, or his nominee.

1.20 The Act seeks as far as possible to avoid the difficulties of imposing corporate criminal responsibility by use of the much-criticized attribution test—and this is certainly avoided by use of section 7. However where the attribution test is successfully applied, and criminal liability for an offence under sections 1, 2 or 6 is attributed to a body corporate, criminal liability does not end there. Section 14 provides that a senior officer (defined by section 14(4)) who consented to or connived in the offence committed by the body corporate is liable to prosecution for the same offence.

1.21 Greater clarity on the position of corporations and their vulnerability to the activities of senior officers and subsidiaries must await the present deliberations of the Law Commission. In the meantime the test of criminal liability for companies for offences under sections 1, 2, and 6 will have to make use of the attribution test and the search for the 'controlling mind'.

1.22 Individuals guilty of offences under sections 1, 2, and 6 face up to 10 years in prison and/or an unlimited fine. Corporations convicted of any of the offences face an unlimited fine. In addition, companies and individuals will be subject upon conviction to the confiscation provisions of the Proceeds of Crime Act 2002 and, perhaps more worryingly for many, automatic mandatory debarment from public works contracts for an indefinite period. At the time of writing, it is a moot point whether a conviction under section 7 will be interpreted as a judgment that triggers Article 45 of the Public Procurement Directive.[1]

1.23 Companies whose business has led them to introduce codes of conduct in line with the Foreign Corrupt Practices Act 1977 of the United States, would do well to study the ways in which the UK Act goes further that its US counterpart. For example, where the latter has a tolerance for some facilitation payments, the UK Act has none. The UK Act punishes both the giver and receiver of the bribe, and of course

---

[1] Council Directive (EC) 2004/18 on the coordination of procedures for the award of public works contracts, public supply contracts and public service contracts [2004] OJ L134/114.

covers all forms of domestic bribery, not simply the corruption of foreign public officials.

The Act amends the law on consents to prosecution, substituting for the Attorney   1.24
General (in section 10) the Director of Public Prosecutions, the Director of the Serious Fraud Office, and the Director of the Revenue and Customs Prosecution Office. It is to be both hoped and anticipated that the protocol that will be published (updating that which has served hitherto) will demonstrate a harmonious approach to decision-making.

The Act will come into force on a date to be appointed, which is unlikely to be   1.25
before April 2011.

At the time of writing there is an active public debate about how bribery by   1.26
business should be sanctioned—whether, for example, the emphasis should be upon administrative fines and disgorgement, saving time and money and avoiding the risks of debarment, or whether bribery is so serious that only prosecution and the realistic fear of it will suffice to deter the delinquents. Both the Serious Fraud Office (SFO) and the Financial Services Authority (FSA) have taken an interest in the subject, with the former being detailed as the lead prosecutor. The policy of the SFO in both encouraging companies to own up and cooperate and its own policy of cooperation with overseas agencies, have been the subject of judicial scrutiny at the highest level. This has extended to the use of plea bargaining procedures originally designed to encourage accomplices to inform on their former organized crime associates.

Section 9 guidance may help to inform decision-making, allowing those who   1.27
advise both companies and individuals safely to predict outcomes. Unfortunately, for the time being uncertainty is further increased by the uncertain fate of both the SFO and FSA.

What is nonetheless apparent is a determination on the part of governments here   1.28
and elsewhere to encourage compliance with the best commercial ethical standards and, in appropriate circumstances, to punish those who fall below those standards. Therefore, bribing one's way to commercial success is clearly to be avoided and companies anxious to avoid even the opprobrium that comes with the investigation will doubtless turn to their legal advisers in an effort to avoid such an unwelcome outcome.

In conclusion, the Act is straightforward; its enforcement will depend heavily on   1.29
the exercise of fair and proportionate prosecutorial discretion and ultimately on the common sense of juries and the clarity of judicial instruction.

2

BACKGROUND

A. THE PROBLEM OF CORRUPTION

1. Identifying the Problem: Incidents of Corruption

(a) *Public sector corruption*

Corruption at national and local government level, or even in qausi-autonomous non-governmental organizations, has undoubtedly diminished in the century and a quarter since the first piece of legislation was passed to prevent it. Judicial corruption is almost unheard of in this country: 'Judges in the United Kingdom have an international reputation for being independent, impartial and highly ethical, and judicial corruption is extremely rare'.[1]   2.01

What does make the headlines is corruption in the police force, in local government, and occasionally nationally. On 3 November 1993, Gordon Foxley, former head of defence procurement at the Ministry of Defence with oversight of the procurement of fuses and ammunition from arms manufacturers, was convicted of 12 counts of corruption contrary to section 1 of the Prevention of Corruption Act 1906. Each count alleged receipt by him of a secret and corrupt payment from one of three foreign arms manufacturers. On 26 May 1994, he was sentenced by His Honour Judge Brookes to a four-year jail sentence, comprising four years on each count to be served concurrently. In February 1997, Michael Allcock, a senior tax inspector in the Special Compliance Office, was convicted on six counts of corruptly accepting money and other benefits from taxpayers between 1987 and 1992 in return for favourable treatment of their tax affairs. He was sentenced to five years' imprisonment. Nonetheless, the problem remains serious enough to give rise to a significant number of prosecutions each year and equally a need for clear and enforceable laws.   2.02

---

[1] 'Evaluation Report on the United Kingdom', adopted by the Group of States against Corruption (GRECO) at its Sixth Plenary Meeting, Strasbourg, 10–14 September 2001, as cited in Transparency International, *Global Corruption Report 2007*.

(b) *Private sector corruption*

2.03   The focus of the Transparency International *Global Corruption Report 2009* was private sector corruption. While not a widespread concern in the United Kingdom, the report recognized that domestic corruption in the private sector is not unheard of. In March 2008, the police investigated allegations that a senior manager of transportation contractor Metronet awarded contracts worth £850,000 (US$1.26 million) to refurbish London's Oxford Circus subway station to a company with which he had close business links and which appeared to be totally unqualified to undertake the project. Surveys have highlighted concerns about corruption in specific industry sectors. For example, a 2006 survey of corruption in the UK construction industry undertaken by the Chartered Institute of Building (CIOB) revealed that:

- 41 per cent of respondents had been offered a bribe at least once;
- 41 per cent of 335 construction professionals think that corruption is widespread;
- 56 and 57 per cent of respondents feel that bribery to obtain planning permission and contracts, respectively, are serious problems;
- more than two-thirds feel that the UK construction industry is not doing enough to tackle corruption; and
- three-quarters do not feel that the UK Government is doing enough to tackle the problem.

(c) *Foreign bribery*

2.04   Recent surveys indicate varying levels of awareness and attitudes in the UK business community towards corruption. KPMG's 2007 *Overseas Bribery and Corruption Survey* revealed that a large majority of respondents were aware that, under the UK Anti-Terrorism, Crime and Security Act 2001, UK citizens can be prosecuted for an act of bribery committed wholly overseas. Of these respondents, however, almost one-third said that they had taken no action to communicate this to their employees. Half of these respondents said that they 'did not think it was relevant to their business'. Surveys by Control Risks and Simmons & Simmons show that awareness of UK laws against foreign bribery may be decreasing over time. In 2002, the year the Act came into force, 68 per cent of respondents said that they were familiar with its main points. By 2006, only 28 per cent said that they had detailed knowledge of the law, and 48 per cent were totally ignorant of it. According to the same survey, approximately 90 per cent of UK respondents had adopted codes explicitly addressing bribery and facilitation payments. A survey by PricewaterhouseCoopers in 2008 found a similar incidence of anti-bribery codes in UK companies, but it also found that fewer than one-quarter of respondents were confident that these codes significantly mitigate corruption risks.

2. The Scale of the Problem: Measuring Corruption

2.05   While several large-scale research initiatives measure and compare corruption within and across countries, its clandestine nature makes it virtually impossible to assess with any degree of accuracy. On a broad-brush basis, the World Bank estimated that around $1 trillion is paid each year in bribes to public officials and office holders. Corruption itself leads to unquantifiable damage to the legitimate economy, undermining democratic institutions and wreaking immeasurable social harm.

Transparency International's Corruption Data gives, so far as is possible, a 'snap-shot' of the scale of the problem: 2.06

Measure of corruption	Source
$1 trillion worth of bribes paid each year	The World Bank
25% of African states' GDP lost per year, equating to approximately $148 billion per year	U4 Anti-corruption Resource Centre, 2007
Losses to corruption equal 20%–40% of Official Development Assistance	The World Bank, *StAR Report*, 2007
400% GDP gain from fighting corruption	The World Bank
Corruption accelerates the depletion of natural resources, notably primary forests and inshore fishing grounds, which many communities rely on for their livelihoods	United Nations Development Programme (UNDP) report, *Accelerating Human Development in Asia and the Pacific*, 2008
0.5 to 1.0 percentage point drag on economic growth	The World Bank
One-quarter of UK-based international companies surveyed in 2006 said that they had lost business to corrupt competitors in the last 5 years	Control Risks
In developing countries, corruption raises the cost of connecting a household to a water network by as much as 30%, inflating the cost of achieving the Millennium Development Goals on water and sanitation by more than US $48 billion or nearly half of annual global aid outlays	Transparency International, *Global Corruption Report 2008*
In the United Kingdom, the National Health Service's anti-fraud unit reported in 2006 that it had stopped corruption totalling more than £170 million (US $300 million) since 1999	Transparency International, *Global Corruption Report 2006*

3. The Effect of the Problem

'Corruption is an insidious plague that has a wide range of corrosive effects on society. It under-   2.07
mines democracy and the rule of law, leads to violations of human rights, distorts markets, erodes the quality of life and allows organised crime, terrorism and other threats to human security to flourish. This evil phenomenon is found in all countries—big and small, rich and poor . . . corruption hurts the poor disproportionately by diverting funds intended for development, undermining a government's ability to provide basic services, feeding inequality and injustice and discouraging foreign aid and investment. Corruption is a key element in economic under-performance and a major obstacle to poverty alleviation and development.'[2]

---

[2] Kofi-Annan, former Secretary General, United Nations, in his foreword to the 2004 UN Convention Against Corruption.

The proceeds of corruption corrupt others in so far as they must be laundered through the banking system and into the legitimate economy. Treasuries are looted, tax revenues denied, useless and unfinished infrastructures are created, while whole communities remain deprived of the basics of life, such as clean water, shelter, food, and medicines.

4. The Movement for Reform

2.08 The United Kingdom was one of the earliest signatories of the OECD Convention but was then heavily criticized by pressure groups, including Transparency International, for domestic laws that did not appear to coincide with the Convention's requirements. In its detailed examination, the Bribery Working Group of the OECD put it this way:

> [there is] a lack of clarity among the different legislative and regulatory instruments in place . . . The current substantive law governing bribery in the UK is characterised by complexity and uncertainty.[3]

2.09 In a ringing endorsement of the OECD's criticism, the Law Commission described the UK law of bribery as 'riddled with uncertainty and in need of rationalisation'.[4]

2.10 Over the past 15 years, the movement for reform has gained considerable momentum. The Bribery Act 2010—the Government's latest attempt at reform—represents a concise and sound basis of agreement between the various groups that have long-dominated the debate.

2.11 The extensive consultation and review period, and cross-party support for legislative amendment, eased the Bill's passage through Parliament. It is hoped that the Act will deliver a modern and comprehensive law, with an outcome to which all interested parties can subscribe.

B. DEVELOPMENT OF DOMESTIC LAW

1. Common Law

'the common law . . . abhors corruption'[5]

2.12 Throughout the centuries of its operation, opinions fluctuated as to whether bribery at common law, now to be abolished along with its statutory fellows,[6] was to be regarded either as a general offence or made up of individual offences distinguished by the office

---

[3] OECD, *Phase 2 Report on Implementation of the OECD Anti-Bribery Convention*, March 2005.
[4] Law Commission, *Reforming Bribery* (Law Com No 313, 2008).
[5] *R v Whitaker* [1914] 3 KB 1283.
[6] Section 17 of the Bribery Act 2010.

or function involved. D Lanham, in *Criminal Law: Essays in Honour of JC Smith*,[7] noted that, '[T]he offence underwent a development over the centuries and is often described in terms of a number of individual offences rather than a single offence'. Successive Law Commission Reports have cited examples of specific offences, or specific instances of the offence, such as bribery of a privy councillor[8] and bribery of a coroner.[9]

Russell on Crime[10] assisted with the following general statement: 2.13

Bribery is the receiving or offering [of] any undue reward by or to any person whatsoever, in a public office, in order to influence his behaviour in office, and incline him to act contrary to the known rules of honesty and integrity.

The common law offence of bribery was limited to public sector corruption and   2.14
depended on the bribee holding a 'public office'. It was an indictable-only offence with no statutory limit in terms of imprisonment.

The elements of the common law offence were as follows: 2.15

(1) receiving or offering

(2) undue reward

(3) to a person in a public office

(4) to influence and

(5) incline him to act contrary to rules of honesty and integrity.

(a) *Public office*

Those involved in the administration of justice could commit the common   2.16
law offence of bribery, such as a juror in *R v Young*,[11] a justice in *R v Gurney*,[12] and a coroner in *R v Harrison*.[13] Prosecutions were also been initiated against a Lord Chancellor in *R v Bacon*[14] and *R v Earl of Macclesfield*,[15] a chief justice in *Thorpe's Case*,[16] a police constable in *R v Richardson*,[17] and a First Lord of the Treasury in *R v Vaughan*.[18]

---

[7] Edited by Peter Smith (London: Butterworths, 1987) 92–93.
[8] *Vaughan* (1769) 4 Burr 2494, 98 ER 308.
[9] *Harrison* (1800) 1 East PC 382.
[10] JW Cecil Turner (London: Stevens, 12th edn, 1964).
[11] (1801) 2 East 14.
[12] (1867) 10 Cox 550.
[13] (1800) 1 East PC 382.
[14] (1620) 2 State Tr 1087.
[15] (1775) 16 State Tr 767.
[16] (1775) 16 State Tr 767.
[17] 111 Cent Crim Ct Sess Pap 612.
[18] (1769) 4 Burr 2494.

2.17   The most widely cited definition of who was to be regarded as a public officer for the purposes of common law bribery can be extracted from the case of *R v Whitaker*,[19] in which 'a public officer' was defined as:

> . . . an officer who discharges any duty in the discharge of which the public are interested, more clearly so if he is paid out of a fund provided by the public. If taxes go to supply his payment and the public have an interest in the duties he discharges, he is a public officer.

(b) *Intention to influence*

2.18   To be guilty of an offence at common law, the payer must have intended to influence the behaviour of the public officer and incline him to act 'contrary to the known rules of honesty and integrity'. In *R v Gurney*[20] this mental element was held to include an intention to produce any effect at all on the decision of a public officer.

(c) *Any undue reward*

2.19   Case law suggests that entertainment and treats when of small value were not prohibited under the common law because they could not be regarded as having been conferred in order to influence a person, or incline him to act contrary to the known rules of honesty and integrity.[21] In the *Bodmin Case*,[22] Willes J stated that he had been required to swear that he would not take any gift from a man who had a plea pending, unless it was 'meat or drink, and that of small value':

> . . . That is not a mere form, chanted ancient times; it is as much as to express that the law will trust even a person who may have to decide upon the lives and properties of others to take, but only in the form of refreshment, which is to be consumed at the moment and not pocketed or reserved for future enjoyment, small quantities of meat and drink. Moreover, it is an illustration of that saying, which is quite familiar to Lawyers, that the law deals with substance and not with shadows. The law allows those trivial matters which occur from time to time, and cannot be prevented, which really do no mischief except in the minds of the suspicious; no inferences to be drawn against a person who simply eats or drinks in the way of moderate refreshment. Well, now. I am quite conscious that, that which might present attractions to one man which he could not resist may to another appear possible to avoid. A hungry creature will go into the trap for a bait, at which the well-fed one will turn up his nose with disdain. But it must be obvious (I have said enough, and I meant no more in what I said than to introduce what really is at the bottom of the decision in all these cases) that the Judge must satisfy his mind whether that which was done was really done in so unusual and suspicious a way that he ought to impute to the person who has done it a criminal intention in doing it, or whether the circumstances are such that it may fairly be imputed to the man's generosity, or to his profusion, or to his desire to express his good will to those who honestly help his cause without resorting to the illegal means of attracting voters by means of an appeal to their appetites.

---

[19] [1914] 3 KB 1283.
[20] (1867) 10 Cox CC 550.
[21] *Woodward v Maltby* [1959] VR 794.
[22] (1869) 1 O'M & H 121.

(d) *The defence of duress*

The common law defences of duress by threats and duress of circumstances apply   2.20
to offences of bribery at common law and to offences under the Prevention of
Corruption Acts.

(e) *Extra-territorial jurisdiction of the common law offence of bribery*

For the purpose of any common law offence of bribery, from 14 February 2002[23] it   2.21
was immaterial if the functions of the person who received or was offered a reward
had no connection with the United Kingdom and were carried out in a country or
territory outside the United Kingdom.[24]

(f) *CPS charging practice*

Common law bribery was not often charged, as there was a substantial overlap   2.22
between this offence and the statutory offences relating to corruption.[25]

(g) *Common law offence of bribery and Members of Parliament*

In 1992 the question of whether the courts have jurisdiction over MPs in respect of   2.23
the common law offence of bribery was decided as a preliminary point as a prelude
to the trial of the then Conservative MP, Harry Greenway. In the event, no trial took
place. Mr Greenway was discharged and therefore no further judicial consideration
was given to the issue. He had been accused of incidents of bribery jointly with
executives of an engineering company which held contracts with British Rail and
was an employer in Mr Greenway's constituency. Buckley J ruled that parliamentary
privilege was no bar to the prosecution of an MP:

I am satisfied that the undoubted common law offence of bribery is not artificially limited by
reference to any particular shade of meaning of the word 'office'. The underlying reason or principle is concerned with the corruption of those who undertake a duty, in the proper discharge of
which the public is interested. . . . That a Member of Parliament against whom there is a prima
facie case of corruption should be immune from prosecution in the courts of law is to my mind
an unacceptable proposition at the present time. I do not believe it to be the law.

The case never proceeded to a full trial, since in a separate trial of the company   2.24
executives the judge ruled that there was no case to answer and the Crown later
offered no evidence against Mr Greenway.

---

[23] Anti-terrorism, Crime and Security Act 2001 (Commencement No 3) Order 2002, SI 2002/228.
[24] Anti-Terrorism, Crime and Security Act 2001, s 108.
[25] See CPS Legal Guidance on Bribery and Corruption, available at <http://www.cps.gov.uk/legal/a_to_c/
bribery_and_corruption/#P65_5220> (last visited 29 June 2010).

2. Public Bodies Corrupt Practices Act 1889

2.25   The Public Bodies Corrupt Practices Act 1889 was introduced in the wake of revelations of corrupt practice made before a Royal Commission appointed to inquire into the affairs of the Metropolitan Board of Works.[26]

2.26   Established in 1885,[27] the Metropolitan Board of Works exercised all the powers of local government in London. Financial controls were exercised by the Commissioners for Works, where more than £50,000 was involved, and by Parliament, where more than £100,000 was involved.[28] In October and November 1886, the *Financial News* published two articles criticizing the Board's method of disposing of surplus land.

2.27   In 1887, the Board itself appointed a Select Committee to enquire into allegations of corruption in the sale of land. The Committee made little headway (the accusers refused to give evidence and the Board had no power to compel them to do so) and, in March 1888, its function was superseded by the establishment of a Royal Commission (see below).

2.28   In the autumn of 1887 there was a general clamour from the London vestries and district boards for a government investigation into the disposal of surplus lands, and in December the Board resolved that in future such disposals should in the first instance be submitted to public auction. Nevertheless, the accusations continued. The *Daily Chronicle*, for example, asserted that the ratepayers had been defrauded of £57,000 in a single transaction in Shaftesbury Avenue, and in February 1888 Lord Randolph Churchill successfully proposed a motion in the House of Commons for the appointment of a Royal Commission to enquire into the workings of the Board.[29]

2.29   Its findings confirmed that the Board had repeatedly failed to invite public competition for the sale and lease of premises and that premises so disposed of were often vested in pauper owners who were the nominees of Board members. It also reported that payments had been received from tenants found for public houses, and that bribes had been taken by the Board in its capacity as music hall censor. The Commission recommended:

> that it would be well if it were made a criminal offence to offer any member or official of a public body any kind of payment or reward in relation to the affairs of the body of which he is a member and also if the person accepting it were made amenable to the criminal law.[30]

2.30   In 1888, 'on Motion of Lord Randolph Churchill, [a] Bill for the more effectual prevention and punishment of Bribery and Corruption of and by members, officers,

---

[26] Fennell and Thomas, *Corruption in England and Wales: an Historical Analysis* (Department of Law, University College, Cardiff, 1983).

[27] Metropolis Local Management Act 1885.

[28] See n 26 above.

[29] FHW Sheppard, 'Shaftesbury Avenue', *Survey of London: volumes 31 and 32: St James Westminster, Part 2* (1963) 68–84.

[30] See n 26 above.

or servants of corporations, councils, boards, commissions, or other public bodies, ordered to be brought in by Lord Randolph Churchill, Sir Robert Fowler, Mr. Jennings, Mr. Whitbread, Sir Henry James, and Mr. Richard Power' was introduced to Parliament.

Apparent throughout all 'negotiations' during the Bill's passage was the overwhelming desire to see the Bill succeed, and to succeed by dealing with the specific 'evils' the Royal Commission had identified. That commentators found it unambitious[31] is not surprising in that context. By way of example, in the House of Commons debates on 14 March 1889, one MP noted, 'I do not doubt that if the Government support it in the other House the matter will go through if we insist upon it. I should not like the Bill to be endangered'. The Bill's sponsor, Lord Randolph Churchill, even went so far as to respond to calls for a widening of the Bill's scope: 2.31

I fear that if the scope of the Bill were extended no progress would be made with any legislation on the subject. There is an essential difference between a private body and a public one. A private body has a direct interest in looking after its own servants, but in the case of a public body what is everybody's business is nobody's business, and thus public bodies become engaged in transactions which the members in their private capacity would not contemplate for a moment. At some time, perhaps, Parliament may take into consideration the mischievous practice of giving commissions and tips of all kinds; but it is too much to attempt now. The Bill is the direct offspring of the Commission to inquire into the Metropolitan Board. The Commission found that persons had been guilty of corrupt practices for which they could not be got hold of in any way. I may mention that I have received a large number of letters from Corporations and persons connected with public bodies approving the Bill, and these letters throw a lurid light upon the prevalence of practices which this Bill may do something to prevent in the future.

The 1889 Act had a total of 10 sections. The Act provided:[32] 2.32

(1) Every person who shall by himself or by or in conjunction with any other person, corruptly solicit or receive, or agree to receive, for himself, or for any other person, any gift, loan, fee, reward, or advantage whatever as an inducement to, or reward for, or otherwise on account of any member, officer, or servant of a public body as in this Act defined, doing or forbearing to do anything in respect of any matter or transaction whatsoever, actual or proposed, in which the said public body is concerned, shall be guilty of an offence.

(2) Every person who shall by himself or by or in conjunction with any other person corruptly give, promise, or offer any gift, loan, fee, reward, or advantage whatsoever to any person, whether for the benefit of that person or of another person, as an inducement to or reward for or otherwise on account of any member, officer, or servant of any public body as in this Act defined, doing or forbearing to do anything in respect of any matter or transaction whatsoever, actual or proposed, in which such public body as aforesaid is concerned, shall be guilty of an offence.

[31] See, eg, ibid.
[32] Section 1.

(a) *The bribe: 'gift, loan, fee, reward, or advantage'*

2.33 The terms 'gift', 'loan', 'fee', and 'reward' were not defined. 'Advantage' included any office or dignity, and any forbearance to demand any money or money's worth or valuable thing, and included any aid, vote, consent, or influence, or pretended aid, vote, consent, or influence, and also included any promise or procurement of or agreement or endeavour to procure, or the holding out of any expectation of any gift, loan, fee, reward, or advantage, as before defined.

2.34 The bribe must have acted as an inducement to, a reward for, or otherwise on account of any public officer doing or forbearing to do anything in respect of a matter concerning his office.

(b) *A 'public body'*

2.35 As originally enacted, the 1889 Act was concerned only with local public bodies in the United Kingdom, meaning any council of a county or county of a city or town, any council of a municipal borough, any board, commissioners, select vestry, or other body which had power to act under and for the purposes of any Act relating to local government, or the public health, or to poor law or otherwise to administer money raised by rates in pursuance of any public general Act. Section 4(2) of the Prevention of Corruption (Amendment) Act 1916 extended this definition to encompass 'local and public authorities of all descriptions'.

3. Prevention of Corruption Act 1906

2.36 The march towards the statutory regime only now to be repealed can be traced to correspondence in *The Times* newspaper beginning in December 1876, with a reference to the case of *Coe v Southern*. This litigation concerned a stage manager alleged to have received half the fees paid by actors to agents for securing engagements.[33] *The Times*, in its issue of 13 July 1877, summed up the correspondence thus:

First came solicitors accused of betraying the trust of their employers, and leaguing with third parties to divide fees to which they had no sort of just claim. . . . Then followed bankers, auctioneers, architects, insurance agents, and accountants. There does not seem, in short, to be any end to the ramifications of this canker which has grown to such a height as to threaten the extinction of honest plain-dealing altogether. It may be traced, indeed, through a much wider ramification than the correspondence we have published has as yet disclosed, and through all shades of questionableness, from direct bribery of the most corrupt kind, such as that of the architect or engineer who receives douceurs from the contractors and tradesmen whom he is bound to overlook, to the more venal, but still not justifiable, gifts or 'discounts,' or 'half commissions,' which nominally unpaid agents, such as bankers, may receive from a broker. What is essentially the same kind of thing may be traced in the commissions offered to clergymen and schoolmasters for introducing hymnals or school-books among their congregations or pupils, in the 'discounts' which tradesmen allow schoolmasters on the bills which they pay for pupils, and generally in the fees exacted or expected in almost every branch of trade for what is called 'introducing' business. The shipbroking

---

[33] Albert Crew, *The Law Relating To Secret Commissions And Bribes (Christmas Boxes, Gratuities, Tips, Etc. The Prevention Of Corruption ACT, 1906)* (1913) (with foreword by Sir Edward Fry).

trade is honeycombed with the same evil which pervades stockbroking, and secret discounts are exacted on freights. . . . Look where we will we find traces of the evil more or less pronounced, more or less evincing lax morals, and a corrupt method of doing business. . . .

The next best thing to abolishing the commission system altogether is clearly to make it a public thing in all cases; and where paid professional agents such as solicitors, engineers, and architects are concerned, it might perhaps be made criminal to take these fees in secret. These suggestions are all more or less feeble, however, in view of the terrible strength of the actual state of things, and we can only hope now that public attention has been roused to the gravity of the mischief it will not go to sleep again till something is done to check its further spread. The commercial prosperity of England is wrapped up in the probity which the practices under review are rapidly making a thing of the past.

In 1896, after this outpouring of concern over secret commissions, the London Chamber of Commerce appointed a special committee to investigate its prevalence. Its report was published in May 1898. Among other findings: 2.37

Your Committee conclude from the evidence before them that secret commissions in various forms are prevalent in almost all trades and professions to a great extent, and that in some trades the practice has increased, and is increasing, and they are of opinion that the practice is producing great evil, alike to the morals of the commercial community and to the profits of honest traders.

Bribes in all forms, including secret commissions, owe their existence sometimes to the desire of the donor to obtain the assistance of the donee: sometimes to the demand expressed or implied of the donee that the bribe shall be given.

In the first class of cases your Committee have reason to believe that the bribe is often given unwillingly and with a pang of conscience, as the result of the keen competition in trade, and in the fear, too often well founded, that unless given other less scrupulous rivals will obtain an advantage; many cases have come before your Committee in which traders have believed (often though not perhaps always without reason) that their entire failure to obtain orders has been due to the want of a bribe.

The second class of cases are those in which the recipient extorts the bribe from those who have established business relations with his principal. This practice is rendered more effective and oppressive by a combination between the blackmailers. The servant or agent who demands a commission and fails to receive it, not infrequently warns his fellows in the same position in the trade against the honest trader, who thus finds himself shut out from dealings with a whole circle of firms.

The bribes given naturally take many forms; most generally they are given in the simple form of a money payment, the worst form of which is a pro rata commission on the business done; sometimes in the shape of a loan, which places the borrower at the absolute mercy of the lender, who, if he be dissatisfied with the amount of custom he receives, can call in, or threaten to call in, the loan; sometimes the bribe consists of presents of plate, wine or other things, and not infrequently it is administered in the form of lavish hospitality and treating.

. . .

The mass of corruption which the evidence before the Committee shows to exist may appear to some persons so great and complex as to render it hopeless to struggle towards purity. Your Committee do not take this view of the matter. They believe that the discussion of the subject and the publicity of some cases before the Law Courts have already done some good; and they recall the undoubted fact that corruption formerly existed in this country in regions where it is now entirely unknown; that there are cases in past times in which bribery threw a stain upon occupants of the Bench; that at one time a large number of the members of the House of Commons were in the pay of the Crown; and that commissions and other secret forms of bribery abounded in Government departments. Your Committee accept the improvement which has taken place in these directions in the last fifty years as a fact full of encouragement for the commercial community of Great Britain.

. . .

But meanwhile, and independently of legislation, it appears to your Committee that much may be done if only the community will rouse themselves to the task.[34]

2.38   This report subsequently formed the basis of several attempts to introduce legislation to combat the 'great evil'. Ultimately, the report called for the criminal law of corruption to be extended into the private sector.

2.39   Lord Chief Justice Russell and Sir Edward Fry introduced the Illicit Secret Commissions Bill. Running to 23 clauses, the Bill successfully passed through its stages in the House of Lords, but failed in the House of Commons because it was thought to be too radical. Modern efforts by legislators to draft a Bill capable of satisfying both Houses and all interested parties are an echo of the efforts of the legislators at the turn of the twentieth century, when two more attempts at introducing Bills to criminalize private bribery were defeated in the Commons.

2.40   On 3 March 1905, Lord Halsbury, then Lord Chancellor, introduced another Bill, this time on behalf of the Government. Much time was taken up in debating the meaning of 'corruptly'; equally, the requirement that the fiat of the Attorney General should be required was hotly debated.[35] Without it, it was feared that the Act would be become a blackmailer's charter. However, to secure the passing of the Bill, the condition was eventually retained. Royal Assent was given in 1906, and the Prevention of Corruption Act came into force on 1 January 1907.

(a) *Corruption in the private sector*

2.41   Extending the law of corruption into the private sector, section 1(1) of the 1906 Act provides:

If any agent corruptly accepts or obtains, or agrees to accept or attempts to obtain, from any person, for himself or for any other person, any gift or consideration as an inducement or reward for doing or forbearing to do, or for having after the passing of this Act done or forborne to do, any act in relation to his principal's affairs or business, or for showing or forbearing to show favour or disfavour to any person in relation to his principal's affairs or business; or if any person corruptly gives or agrees to give or offers any gift or consideration to any agent as an inducement or reward for doing or forbearing to do, or for having after the passing of this Act done or forborne to do, any act in relation to his principal's affairs or business, or for showing or forbearing to show favour or disfavour to any person in relation to his principal's affairs or business . . . he shall be guilty [of an offence].

---

[34] Secret Commissions Committee, 1898.
[35] See n 33 above.

The bribe: 'any gift or consideration' The expression 'consideration' is defined as 2.42
including 'valuable consideration of any kind'. 'Gift' is not defined.

An 'agent' 'Agent' is defined as 'any person employed by or acting for another', 2.43
including a person serving under the Crown or any local or public authority.

It is unclear whether police officers, judicial officers, and local councillors can be 2.44
classified as 'agents' for the purposes of the 1906 Act, though in such cases there may
be recourse to the common law or the 1889 Act. It is also doubtful whether a person
merely purporting to be an agent will suffice for the 1906 Act.

4. Prevention of Corruption Act 1916

Thus, upon its introduction as a statutory crime, the offence of bribery was charac- 2.45
terized, as it was to remain for the next century or more, by the model of master and
servant or principal and agent. The lack of definition of the word 'corruptly', and
the fetter on prosecutions arising from the need for the Attorney General's consent,
were among the more controversial measures that the Law Commission had to
re-think before it could modernize the statutory crime of corruption in the public
or the private sector. To these was added a further complication introduced at break-
neck speed by the Prevention of Corruption Act 1916 to deal with the scandal of
bribery in the procurement of war supplies. Parliament enacted a presumption
of guilt, shifting the burden of proof in given circumstances to the defence.

At the Bill's second reading the Home Secretary, Herbert Samuel, opened the 2.46
debate as follows:

This Bill is designed to strengthen the law against corruption. Public attention was drawn to this
matter recently by the case against officials of the Royal Army Clothing Department, who were
charged with corruption and receiving bribes from contractors to induce them to pass certain
goods which it was their duty to inspect. In passing sentence upon those offenders, the learned
judge who tried the case used these words: 'I should like to add this, as a respectful suggestion to
the Legislature, that it is high time that a short measure should be passed giving power to the
Courts, at all events during the continuance of the War, to inflict on persons convicted of bribery
or attempting to bribe Government employee's a long period of penal servitude, because the
penalties provided by the Corruption Act are absolutely useless and inadequate to deal with
matters of this sort.'

The House will agree that these offences are of a kind most dangerous to the State. If corruption
in any degree spreads among Government officials, the body politic is affected with weakness in
all forms of its activities. We are very happy to think that hitherto our public service has been in
the main remarkably free from corruption, and this House will desire to take any measures that
may be necessary and well devised to ensure the continuance of that state of things, and to penalise
individuals here and there who may have acted on a lower standard of honesty and public duty
than the rest.[36]

---

[36] HC, vol 86, col 1633 (31 October 1916).

2.47   The Bill was rapidly passed through Parliament as an emergency measure, becoming law on 22 December 1916. Attempts by Sir Albert Spicer to resurrect the abandoned clause 3 (abolition of the need for the Attorney General's consent)[37] failed and did nothing to halt the progress of the Bill.

2.48   The Act increased the maximum sentence for bribery in relation to contracts with the Government or public bodies, and broadened the definition of a 'public body'.

(a) *The presumption of corruption*

2.49   The 1916 Act provides that:

> Where in any proceedings against a person for an offence under the Prevention of Corruption Act 1906, or the Public Bodies Corrupt Practices Act 1889, it is proved that any money, gift, or other consideration has been paid or given to or received by a person in the employment of [Her] Majesty or any Government Department or a public body by or from a person, or agent of a person, holding or seeking to obtain a contract from [Her] Majesty or any Government Department or public body, the money, gift, or consideration shall be deemed to have been paid or given and received corruptly as such inducement or reward as is mentioned in such Act unless the contrary is proved.

2.50   The presumption shifted the burden of proof so that it is for the defence to prove (on a balance of probabilities) that a given payment was not corrupt. It applies only to payments made to employees of the Crown, government departments, or public bodies, and only to cases involving contracts.

2.51   Section 2 of the 1916 Act states that if the prosecution proves that any money, gift or other consideration has been received by a public official, it shall be deemed to have been paid or received corruptly unless the contrary is proved. Since the word 'corruptly' is at the core of the offence, the 1916 Act, on its face, appears to violate Article 6(2) of the European Convention on Human Rights.

5. Anti-Terrorism Crime and Security Act 2001

2.52   In the wake of the Government White Paper, *Raising Standards and Upholding Integrity: the Prevention of Corruption*,[38] and after further sniping from the OECD, clauses were added to a post-9/11 piece of legislation. Part 12 of the Anti-Terrorism, Crime and Security Act 2001, which came into force on 14 February 2002, extended the jurisdiction of domestic courts to acts of bribery committed abroad by UK nationals or bodies incorporated under UK law.

2.53   Section 108(1) of the 2001 Act ensured that the common law offence of bribery extended to persons holding public office outside the UK. Section 108 also amended

---

[37] Sir Albert Spicer stated during debate: 'Further, I hope it may be possible in Committee so to enlarge the Bill as to do away with what we think is a real weakness in the Act of 1906—the fiat of the Law Officer of the Crown. That has been a hindrance. I do not think it has worked in the way intended when the Act of 1906 was passed. Same of the highest authorities—judges who have occupied the position of Attorney-General— have been against this fiat, and I hope we shall be able to abolish it'.

[38] CM 4759, June 2000.

the Public Bodies Corrupt Practices Act 1889, the Prevention of Corruption Act 1906, and the Prevention of Corruption Act 1916 to ensure that those Acts covered the bribery and corruption of officials of foreign public bodies, as well as 'agents' (within the meaning of the 1906 Act) of foreign 'principals' (who may be in the public or private sector). Section 109 gave the courts extra-territorial jurisdiction over bribery and corruption offences committed abroad by UK nationals and bodies incorporated under UK law. It enables specified offences,[39] when committed by UK nationals and bodies incorporated under UK law, to be prosecuted here, wherever those offences take place. This section applied to any body incorporated under the law of any part of the United Kingdom. Section 110 stated that the presumption of corruption was not to apply to any offences committed by virtue of the extensions made by Part 12. The reason for this was that the Government did not wish to widen the application of a presumption which it intended to abolish in any event.

At the time it was thought that these provisions were sufficient to bring the United Kingdom into line with the OECD Convention. As will be seen, subsequent criticism took issue with this complacency.

    2.54

C. BACKGROUND TO THE ACT

1. Overview

Probity in local government became a matter of public concern following a scandal centered in north-east England, which became known as the Poulson affair. John Garlick Llewelyn Poulson (1910–1993) was an architect based in Pontefract, West Yorkshire, who built a small architectural practice into a large integrated company employing architects, planners, lawyers, project managers, and other professionals The practice specialized in shopping centres and major town-centre redevelopments. However, the company fell into financial difficulty, and at the bankruptcy hearings in 1972 it became clear that it had been paying bribes to win lucrative contracts. The Metropolitan Police began an investigation, and Poulson and a number of other men were brought to trial. Following a 52-day trial at Leeds Crown Court, which was widely reported in the press, Poulson was convicted on 11 February 1974 of fraud and jailed for five years (later increased to seven years).

    2.55

A Royal Commission on Standards in Public Life ('the Salmon Commission') was set up in 1974. This recommended, amongst other things, that the anti-corruption Acts from 1889 to 1916, insofar as they applied to the public sector, should be modernized and consolidated. However, the Government, under James Callaghan, took no action.

    2.56

---

[39] These are: any common law offence of bribery; the offences under s 1 of the Public Bodies Corrupt Practices Act 1889; and the first two offences under s 1 of the Prevention of Corruption Act 1906 (bribes obtained by or given to agents).

2.57   More public corruption scandals followed, leading to the setting-up of a Committee on Standards in Public Life in May 1995. In making its recommendations, the Committee thought it important that the general principles of public life be restated, namely selflessness, integrity, objectivity, accountability, openness, honesty, and leadership. The Committee's main recommendation in regard to the law of corruption was to request that steps be taken to clarify the law on bribery in relation to the receipt of a bribe by an MP, as recommended by the Salmon Commission, combined with consolidation of the statute law on bribery. These recommendations also led to the Select Committee on Standards in Public Life—charged with considering the Nolan Report[40]—recommending a review of the law on bribery in similar terms.

2.58   Meanwhile, the Government, represented at the OECD Working Party, was charged with fashioning a convention to outlaw the corruption of foreign public officials by supply-side businesses in the Member States of the OECD.

2.59   Aware that the OECD was coming to the end of its deliberations, and with the signing of a convention and agreement on recommendations to tackle the corruption of foreign public officials, the UK Government asked the Law Commission to consider the reform of UK bribery law.

2. Law Commission Report (1998)

2.60   In 1998, the Law Commission highlighted four major defects in UK bribery law. First, it noted that the law was drawn from a multiplicity of sources, including many overlapping common law offences and at least 11 statutes. Much of that legislation was a hasty response to a contemporary problem and, in consequence, was not comprehensive, clear, or consistent. Secondly, the law was dependent on a distinction between *public* and *non-public* bodies. Thirdly, it was difficult to ascertain to whom the legislation applied. Fourthly, it was queried whether the rebuttable presumption of corruption under section 2 of the 1916 Act was compatible with sections 34 and 35 of the Criminal Justice and Public Order Act 1994.

2.61   In summary, the report[41] recommended that:

(1) Corruption should be codified within a single Bill.

(2) The single Bill should remove the distinction between public and non-public bodies, and in particular should abolish the presumption of corruption established by the 1916 Act for 'public' cases.

(3) In order to extend the present law, it should be an offence to act corruptly in the 'hope' or 'expectation' of a bribe, even when no such bribe had been agreed.

---

[40] Committee on Standards in Public Life, *Standards in Public Life*, CM 2850 (1995) ('the Nolan Report').

[41] Law Commission, *Legislating the Criminal Code: Corruption* (3 March 1998).

(4) Bribery should be split into five offences. The first two would cover persons who either corruptly conferred an advantage or corruptly offered to confer an advantage. The second two would cover persons who either corruptly obtained an advantage or corruptly solicited or agreed to obtain an advantage. The final offence would cover persons who performed their functions as agents corruptly.

(5) The Bill should list relevant fiduciary relationships, that is relationships in which one person is an agent and the other is his principal.

(6) Acting corruptly should be defined as acting 'primarily in return for the conferring of an advantage'. This would be subject to a number of defences including acting in return for remuneration from the principal (employer) and acting with the principal's consent.

(7) The offence created by the Bill should be added to the list of Group A offences in Part 1 of the Criminal Justice Act 1993 ('the 1993 Act'). The effect of doing so would be that certain acts of bribery which occurred outside England and Wales would for jurisdictional purposes be deemed to have occurred in England and Wales.

(8) Procurement of a breach of duty through threats or deception should not be included in the law of corruption.

The Government welcomed the report and stated its intention to present a Bill to Parliament, modelled on the Commission's draft, as soon as possible. It also moved to set up an interdepartmental working group to consider the draft Bill.   2.62

3. Draft Corruption Bill (2003)

The draft Corruption Bill[42] was based on the Law Commission draft issued in 1998. The Government agreed with the majority of the recommendations made in the Law Commission's 1998 report. Therefore, subject to a few modifications, the draft Bill presented to Parliament in the 2002–2003 session largely reflected the draft Bill appended to the Commission's report. However, the only major stakeholder that welcomed it was the Rose Committee (composed of senior judges); otherwise, even those who had previously supported the basic scheme were critical of the Bill.   2.63

4. Joint Committee on the Draft Corruption Bill (2003)

A Joint Committee was appointed on 24 March 2003 to reconsider the draft Corruption Bill.[43] The Committee did not dispute the case for reform, but it did have reservations about several aspects of the draft Corruption Bill. Particular concerns were that that some corrupt conduct was not caught; that the general law of corruption was not defined with sufficient clarity; that the definition of corruption   2.64

---

[42] CM 5777 (March 2003).
[43] HL Paper 157 (July 2003).

was too vague for business and could be interpreted in a manner that was inconsistent with the UK's international obligations; that the agent/principal focus was too restrictive; and that the waiver of parliamentary privilege in corruption cases should be narrowed. The written and oral evidence the Committee received was highly critical of the Bill. While no one challenged the need for new legislation, there were many adverse comments on the approach adopted in the Bill and its drafting, clarity, and comprehensibility. The Committee ultimately concluded that the agent/principal focus, which formed the heart of the draft Bill, should be reassessed.

5. Government Response (2003)

2.65 The Government considered at length all of the Committee's conclusions and the recommendations for change.[44] Although making modifications to the definition of corruption to meet some of the issues of clarity and precision brought forward by the Committee itself or in evidence, the Government did not abandon the agent/principal approach proposed by the Law Commission. The Government argued that the Joint Committee's scheme was superficially simpler, but at the expense of omitting any provision on several vital complex situations—notably on advantages given to third parties, and on performing functions corruptly in the hope of a reward. It would also pose greater operational problems—at least in the private sector—because it would cover advantages given independently of any agent/principal relationship.

2.66 Accordingly, no Bill was introduced for consideration by Parliament at that time.

6. Consultation Paper (2005)[45]

2.67 In December 2005, the Home Office again consulted on 'a way forward' from the pre-legislative scrutiny that had defeated the 2003 Draft Bill. Again, it was emphasized that the existing law was fragmented and out of date and needed to be reformed. Consultees were asked eight questions on the following broad areas:

- definitions;
- separation of offences applicable to the public sector from those applicable to the private sector (the majority of consultees opposed such a separation); and
- pre-legislative scrutiny.

2.68 The response to the consultation was published in March 2007. While there was broad support for reform of the Prevention of Corruption Acts, there was no

---

[44] CM 6086 (December 2003).
[45] 'Bribery: Reform of the Prevention of Corruption Acts and SFO Powers in Cases of Bribery of Foreign Officials: a Consultation Paper' (December 2005).

consensus view as to what such reform should be. The consultation showed that there was some degree of support for each of several differing models of reform, but insufficient support for any one particular model to justify its being submitted to Parliament.

In publishing a summary of responses, the Government announced that it had asked the Law Commission to re-examine the law of bribery.   2.69

7. Corruption Bill (2006)

On 23 May 2006, Hugh Bayley MP introduced a Transparency International-sponsored Bill (known thereafter as the 'TI Bill'), having won the support of the House of Commons to introduce it under the 10-minute rule. In June 2006, Downing Street endorsed the Africa All-Party Parliamentary Group's conclusions that the Government should take a lead in tackling international corruption and agreed to implement most of the group's recommendations. The TI Bill thereafter fell away and ceased to feature in the parliamentary programme. To rectify this and to avoid losing important draft legislation, Lord Chidgey brought the Bill forward, updated and amended as a Private Member's Bill, to the House of Lords in November 2006. Whilst not normally TI(UK)'s role to draft parliamentary legislation, it felt compelled to do so on this occasion because of the failure of the Government to place an effective Bill before Parliament.   2.70

This Bill did not proceed, but achieved its purpose of providing impetus to the Government's efforts.   2.71

8. Law Commission Consultation (2007)

On 29 November 2007, the Law Commission published a detailed Consultation[46] to which it received over 30 responses. Its focus was on corruption in the narrow sense of offences relating to bribery—a clear shift that was marked in its terms of reference, which read as follows: 2.72

(1) To review the various elements of the law on bribery with a view to modernisation, consolidation and reform; and to produce a draft Bill. The review will consider the full range of structural options including a single general offence covering both public and private sectors, separate offences for the public and private sectors, and an offence dealing separately with bribery of foreign public officials. The review will make recommendations that:
   (a) provide coherent and clear offences which protect individuals and society and provide clarity for investigators and prosecutors;
   (b) enable those convicted to be appropriately punished;
   (c) are fair and non-discriminatory in accordance with the European Convention on Human Rights and the Human Rights Act 1998; and
   (d) continue to ensure consistency with the UK's international obligations.

---

[46] *Reforming Bribery: A Consultation Paper* (Law Com No 185).

(2) The process used will be open, inclusive and evidence-based and will involve:
   (a) a review structure that will look to include key stakeholders;
   (b) consultation with the public, criminal justice practitioners, academics, parliamentarians, and non-governmental organisations;
   (c) consideration of the previous attempts at reform (including the recent Home Office consultation) and the experiences of law enforcement and prosecutors in using the current law; and
   (d) comparing, in so far as is possible, the experience in England and Wales with that in other countries: this will include making international comparisons, in particular looking at relevant international Conventions and the body of experience around their implementation.
(3) The review will also look at the wider context of corrupt practices to see how the various provisions complement the law of bribery. This will provide the wider context in which the specific reform of bribery law can be considered. This part of the review will comprise a summary of provisions, not recommendations for reform.

2.73 The Consultation Paper prompted significant comment, and ultimately represented a sound basis for agreement between the various interest groups, which have, at different times, dominated the debate.

9. Final Law Commission Report and Draft Bribery Bill (2008)

2.74 The Law Commission's final report was published in October 2008,[47] and had annexed to it a draft Bill, which in due course was forwarded for pre-legislative consideration by the Joint Committee on the Draft Bribery Bill. The report contained the Commission's recommendations for reform, as shaped by the ensuing consultative process. Among other things the Commission proposed:

(1) The repeal of the existing common law and statutory bribery offences and the replacing of them by two general offences of bribing and being bribed (clauses 1 and 2).

(2) The introduction of a specific offence of bribing foreign public officials (clause 4).

(3) The creation of a new criminal offence for companies and partnerships that negligently failed to prevent bribery by persons performing services on their behalf (clauses 5 and 6).

(4) The making of a supplementary provision for the jurisdiction of the offences (clause 7), the application of parliamentary privilege (clause 15), the role of the Attorney General (clause 10), and the powers of the security services (clauses 13 to 14).

---

[47] *Reforming Bribery* (Law Com No 313).

10. Report of the Joint Committee on the Draft Bribery Bill (2009)[48]

The draft Bribery Bill was published by the Ministry of Justice on 25 March 2009   2.75
for pre-legislative scrutiny. The Joint Committee was formed on 11 May 2009, with
a deadline of reporting on the draft Bill by 21 July 2009. The Committee sought a
wide range of evidence to inform its report, hearing oral evidence from 27 witnesses
over a five-week period and receiving a total of 61 written submissions. Among
those who contributed their views were the United Nations (UN), the OECD, the
United States Department of Justice, and several parliamentary select committees
with a long-standing interest in the draft Bill.

The Committee ultimately expressed its strong support for the draft Bribery Bill,   2.76
describing it as 'an important, indeed overdue, step in reforming the United
Kingdom's bribery laws, which have been a source of criticism at home and abroad
for more than thirty years'. Whilst supporting the two proposed offences of bribing
(clause 1) and being bribed (clause 2), together with the 'improper' performance test
developed by the Law Commission and the specific offence of bribing foreign public
officials (clause 4), the Committee was dissatisfied with the draft Bill's focus on
whether a 'responsible person' was negligent, rather than on the collective failure of
the company to ensure that adequate anti-bribery procedures were in place. The
recommendation was therefore for the removal of the need to prove negligence.

While endorsing the substantial penalties available under the legislation, the   2.77
Committee cautioned that the Government had to address the injustice risked by
debarring companies from entering public contracts on an automatic and perpetual
basis. The Committee also endorsed calls for official guidance, particularly on the
meaning of 'adequate procedures'. The Committee deprecated attempts to effect a
piecemeal reform of parliamentary privilege due to the complex constitutional issues
raised that could be better addressed through a future Parliamentary Privileges Bill.
Clause 15 was therefore abandoned.

The Committee agreed with the Government that the Attorney General's respon-   2.78
sibility for directing prosecuting authorities should remain in place without being
reformed by the draft Bill. That being the case, the Committee was satisfied that the
power of consent should be transferred from the Attorney General to the directors
of the prosecuting authorities (enumerated in section 10). The broader reform of the
Attorney General's Office that had been contemplated was deferred when proposed
legislation was lost in the dissolution of Parliament.

The Committee raised concerns about making special provision for the armed   2.79
forces and the intelligence services and this debate continued after the Bill was introduced in the House of Lords and later in the House of Commons. Some thought
that provisions relating to the security and intelligence services should be the subject
of discrete legislation, while others considered that permission to bribe even for
reasons of state and security should nonetheless be subject to parliamentary approval
on a 'per-case' basis. In the end, the Government took the view that a failure to

---

[48] HC 430-I and HL 115-I.

legislate at this stage would provide dangerous lacunae and would jeopardize the position of both the armed forces and security services. Ultimately, its view prevailed.

11. Government's Response[49]

2.80 The Government's response to the Committee's report was published in November 2009. Its contents are not repeated here, but of particular import were the following conclusions.

2.81   The evidence before the Joint Committee suggested that questions relating to what standards should apply, and what factors the jury should take into account, could arise in the absence of any express clarification. Accordingly, the Government's amended Bill ensured that the test of what was expected was a test of what a reasonable person in the United Kingdom would expect.

2.82   On reflection, the Government agreed that there could be a risk that requiring the prosecution to prove negligence might involve unnecessary complexity and have the potential to undermine the broad policy objectives of bringing about a shift away from a corporate culture that was more tolerant of bribery and promoting effective corporate anti-bribery procedures. The Committee's proposed approach was also likely to be more effective in motivating commercial organizations to self-refer bribery disclosed by internal monitoring. The Government therefore accepted the Committee's view that removing the requirement to prove negligence would provide a clearer approach.

2.83   The Government recognized that the meaning of the phrase 'adequate procedures' had to be interpreted in a flexible and proportionate way depending on the size and resources of the company, alongside the ethical risks associated with the industry, geographical area, and the types of transaction concerned and that it must depend on what a commercial organization was doing in practice rather than in theory.

2.84   Given the sensitivities of the time (the MPs' expenses scandal) and the complexities of the issue, the Government decided not to make savings in respect of parliamentary privilege.

2.85   The Bribery Bill 2009 eventually had its first reading in the House of Lords on 19 November 2009, progressing swiftly through both houses to Royal Assent on 8 April 2010.

12. Passage of the Bribery Bill

2.86 The passage of the Bill was marked by extensive debate, a consideration of which is outside of the scope of this text. Practitioners are urged to refer to *Hansard* to chart

---

[49] CM 7748, available at <http://www.justice.gov.uk/publications/docs/draft-bribery-joint-cttee-govt-response.pdf> (last visited 6 July 2010).

the Bill's progress to enactment, having particular regard to governmental pronouncements through the Bill's passage on 'thorny issues' such as facilitation payments and corporate hospitality.

It is submitted that opposition to some of the more controversial provisions were   2.87
stilled not only by a general desire to see a reform of the law, but because legislators felt reassured that there would be no prosecution *blitzkrieg* on British business and that the Government's guidance would assist business to become quickly compliant. Overall, there was an unspoken belief that the UK authorities charged with the investigation and prosecution of bribery would act fairly and proportionately while recognizing that bribery for the benefit of a business which could reasonably have been prevented must not go unpunished.

3

THE GENERAL BRIBERY OFFENCES

A. INTRODUCTION

The Act criminalizes bribery by setting out a number of 'cases' or 'scenarios' to   3.01
describe the conduct being penalized. Section 1 of the Act deals with the activity of
the briber and section 2 with the conduct of the recipient of the bribe. The Act deals
with the criminality of the giver of the bribe and the receiver of the bribe separately.
This distinction not only assists in examining the conduct of any possible suspect
but also sounds in the corporate responsibility offences set out in sections 7 and 8.

The general bribery offences are dependent on being connected to a 'relevant'   3.02
function or activity. The functions or activities must be performed 'improperly', and
in breach of a 'relevant expectation'. These concepts are dealt with in sections 3, 4,
and 5 of the Act.

Under each of the 'cases' or 'scenarios', the prosecution has to prove an *objective*   3.03
test of 'improper' performance based on whether a 'reasonable person' would consider that the bribe was given (in the wider meaning of the Act) or received (in the
wider meaning of the Act) in breach of an expectation of 'good faith' and/or 'impartiality' and/or 'trust' (section 3). Those three concepts are central to the wrong of
bribery itself; they are the defining features of 'improper' conduct.

Knowledge or intention to bring about an improper performance must also be   3.04
proven by the prosecution in three of the six statutory cases under sections 1 and 2
(cases 1 to 3). Of those three cases, two relate to the briber, and one to the receiver.
In the remaining three cases, all concerning the recipient of the bribe, it is irrelevant
whether there is knowledge or belief that the performance of a function/activity is
or will be improper. Similarly, there is no requirement of subjective knowledge or
belief where the bribe is received by a third party on behalf of the receiver.

3.05   Accordingly, when examining conduct to see whether it has or may fall foul of these new general bribery offences, recourse must be had to sections 1, 3, 4, and 5 in the case of payment or potential payment, and to sections 2 to 5 in the case of receipt or potential receipt of a bribe. These sections in turn will have to be considered against the guidance to be published by the Government and finally a judgement will have to be made taking into account all of the circumstances of the case in every case.

3.06   It has been said that the words 'corruptly' or 'with corrupt intent' or 'dishonestly' have been omitted from the Act in pursuit of simplicity, certainty, and effectiveness.[1] That said, it seems inevitable that in the first years of the working of this new legislation, those charged with superintending corporate compliance and ethical behaviour generally may have to have recourse to legal opinion until this legislation becomes more 'user-friendly' through regular use and judicial pronouncements.

B. THE GENERAL BRIBERY OFFENCES

1. The 'Payer'

3.07   Section 1 defines the offence of bribery as it applies to the person who offers, promises, or gives a financial or other advantage to another. That person is referred to in the section as P—he is the payer.

3.08   'Financial or other advantage' is left to be determined as a matter of common sense by the tribunal of fact.[2] The term is in contrast to that used within the 1889 Act, which refers to the offer or acceptance of 'any gift, loan, fee, reward or advantage', whereas the 1906 Act refers to 'any gift or consideration'. It was felt that 'advantage' lends itself to a wide interpretation, capable of encompassing omissions as well as acts, for example.[3] In addition, 'advantage' has been almost universally adopted in a host of Conventions ratified by the UK. These include the OECD Convention against the Bribery of Foreign Public Officials,[4] the United Nations Convention against Corruption,[5] and the Council of Europe's Criminal Law Convention against Corruption.[6]

3.09   Existing definitions of 'advantage' are not consistent and have therefore not been replicated in the new legislation. It is, nevertheless, worthy of note that section 7 of the 1889 Act defined advantage as:

including any office or dignity, and any forbearance to demand any money or money's worth or valuable thing, and includes any aid, vote, consent, or influence, or pretended aid, vote, consent,

---

[1] Joint Committee on the Draft Bribery Bill—First Report.
[2] Explanatory Notes to the Act.
[3] Law Commission Consultation Paper No 185 (October 2007) paras 5.58–5.59.
[4] 'Any undue pecuniary or other advantage' (Art 1).
[5] 'An undue advantage' (Chapter III).
[6] 'An undue advantage' (Chapter II).

or influence, and also includes any promise or procurement of or agreement or endeavour to procure, or the holding out of any expectation of any gift, loan, fee, reward, or advantage, as before defined.

Attempts by the Law Commission to provide a definition resulted in suggestions that were either too complex or unnecessary. The Commission ultimately concluded that definition of the term is unnecessary: '"Advantage" is a term perfectly capable of being understood, in this context, in a common sense way without further elaboration'.

The Law Commission also noted (correctly, it is submitted) that the courts are unlikely to be detained by specious pleas that what seemed advantageous at the time of the transaction (say, a grant of shares) should not be regarded as advantageous in fact, because although unbeknown to P, or to both parties, what was offered turned out to be worthless.[7]   3.10

Section 1 provides that P is guilty of an offence if one of two scenarios (known as 'cases') applies to him. In neither case does it matter whether the advantage is offered, promised, or given by P directly or through a third party.   3.11

(a) Case 1

Case 1 is where—   3.12

(a) P *offers, promises or gives*[8] a financial or other advantage to another person, and

(b) P *intends* the advantage—

   (i) *to induce* a person to perform improperly a relevant function or activity, *or*
   (ii) *to reward* a person for the improper performance of such a function or activity.

It is irrelevant whether the person to whom the advantage is offered, promised, or given is the same person as the person who is to perform, or has performed, the function or activity concerned; responsibility cannot be avoided by the use of intermediaries.   3.13

By using the expression 'offers, promises or gives', the Government has ensured that for either variant of the section 1 offence, the conduct element will be satisfied not only when P in fact confers an advantage on the recipient (R), but also when he represents a willingness to confer an advantage on R. R need do nothing for the offence to be made out. In its final report, the Law Commission recalled that an offer or promise can be implied as well as express. It can be inferred from conduct as well as being given more concrete expression. The Act does not seek to define 'offers, promises or gives' as being words in everyday use which a tribunal of fact will have no difficulty in understanding.   3.14

An example of 'case 1' might be where P is the owner of property A seeking planning advantage which will enhance the value of that property. He commits an   3.15

---

[7] Law Commission, *Reforming Bribery* (Law Com No 313, 2008) para 3.39.

[8] This formulation is in contrast to 'offering' at common law, 'give, promise, or offer' under the 1889 Act, and 'gives or agrees to give or offers' under the 1906 Act.

offence if he offers or gives or promises a sum of money to a council official charged with carrying out a planning function, intending that the council official will perform his functions improperly by failing to demonstrate good faith or impartiality.

3.16 For definitions of 'improper performance' and 'relevant function or activity', applicable in each case irrespective of whether it is an active or passive offence, see below.

(b) *Case 2*

3.17 Case 2 is where—

(a) P offers, promises, or gives a financial or other advantage to another person; and

(b) P knows or believes that the acceptance of the advantage would itself constitute the improper performance of a relevant function or activity.

3.18 This 'case' envisages those circumstances where the person offered or promised or given an advantage, financial or otherwise, would be acting improperly in connection with his function or activity simply by accepting the offer, promise, or gift and that that impropriety is known to P so that the prosecution does not have to prove any specific intent as it does in case 1. See also below where this scenario, as it applies to the recipient, is considered in detail.

3.19 An example would be any significant offer, promise of, or actual gift which is of such significance that its very receipt would place the council or government official in breach of his terms of employment, ie relevant function or activity.

3.20 This section, together with the section 2 case scenarios, will be relevant when considering the Government's guidance on facilitation payments, corporate hospitality, and how the circumstances of the case indicate whether or not there was an improper performance of a relevant function or activity regardless of any secondary motive.

2. The 'Recipient'

3.21 Section 2 defines the offence of bribery as it applies to the recipient or potential recipient of the bribe (R). It distinguishes four cases/scenarios, for which it is irrelevant whether R requests or agrees to receive or accept the advantage directly or through a third party, or whether the advantage is (or is to be) for the benefit of R or another person.

3.22 With the exception of case 3, there is no requirement for the prosecution to prove that R requested, agreed, or received the advantage, with the intention of improperly performing or having another improperly perform a relevant function or activity. Thus, where it can be proved that R requested a bribe and that he did so by promising to perform improperly, the prosecution may choose to assume the burden of proof provided by case 3. Where that burden cannot be discharged, but where it can be shown nonetheless that R improperly requested an advantage or where, having improperly performed a relevant function, R seeks a reward from the beneficiary of that impropriety or improperly performs a relevant function or activity hoping that he might be able to procure a financial or other advantage, then cases 4 to 6 will be preferred.

A number of witnesses giving evidence to the Joint Committee on the Draft Bribery   3.23
Bill described cases 4 to 6 as 'absolute' or strict liability offences, while others contended that the *mens rea* is embedded in the circumstances of the offence. The absence
of a requirement to prove subjective wrongdoing marks a change in the culture in
which taking a bribe is viewed as acceptable. In particular, it is aimed at encouraging
anyone who is expected to act in good faith, impartially, or under a position of trust
to think twice before accepting an advantage for his personal gain. During the Act's
passage, Parliamentary-Under-Secretary of State, Lord Bach, said this:

> R is the best person to understand the expectations to which he or she is subject. If R could avoid
> liability on the ground of lack of mens rea, it would create a significant grey area that might be
> exploited in cases in which the recipient was aware of the expectations that applied, as it would be
> much easier for the recipient to claim ignorance of the fact that his or her conduct constituted a
> breach of an expectation than it would be for a prosecutor to prove that the recipient was aware
> that it did. I hope the House finds helpful the analogy of gross negligence manslaughter. A person
> can be convicted of gross negligence manslaughter regardless of whether they recognised that their
> conduct would amount to a breach of a duty to take care.[9]

Whereas in the Law Commission's original Draft Bill, the model of gross negli-   3.24
gence manslaughter was influential in the drafting, this is perhaps the only place
in which this reasoning survived into the Act itself.

(a) *Case 3*

Case 3 is where R requests, agrees to receive, or accepts a financial or other advantage   3.25
intending that, in consequence, a relevant function or activity should be performed
improperly (whether by R or another person).

This is the only variant of the receipt offence that incorporates a requirement for   3.26
knowledge or intention. In her evidence to the Joint Committee on the Draft
Bribery Bill, the then Attorney General, Baroness Scotland of Asthal, noted that the
purpose of case 3 is to 'fill the vacuum that would otherwise exist under cases 4 to 6
in circumstances where the recipient accepted an advantage while intending (but
not proceeding) to improperly perform their functions'.[10] Case 3 could apply where
the other person had no intention of paying a bribe.

(b) *Case 4*

Case 4 is where: 3.27

(a) R requests, agrees to receive, or accepts a financial or other advantage; and

(b) the request, agreement, or acceptance itself constitutes the improper performance by R of a relevant function or activity.

---

[9] *Hansard*, HL, col 122 (2 February 2010).
[10] Q674.

3.28   In this scenario, the prosecution does not have to prove that R either knew or believed that the performance of the function or activity is improper, simply that it was. In this scenario or 'case', only one act, the request, agreement, or acceptance of the advantage, is required to make out the offence. It would be open to the jury to find that, by virtue only of the position R held, it was improper in and of itself to accept the advantage irrespective of any impact it may have had on R's thinking.

3.29   This section criminalizes the conduct of those persons from whom good faith and/or impartiality and/or fidelity is expected in the performance of the functions to which section 3 relates. It is the very betrayal of those three expectations that constitutes the offence without there being any additional requirement that there be proof of improper performance. As has been pointed out above, this is a cultural shift, making it plain that those performing the functions enumerated in section 3 share a responsibility with those whose conduct is criminalized in section 1 in being alert to the possibility of being suborned and deterred from even contemplating such activity.

3.30   In its final report, the Law Commission emphasized that in some instances it will be the very occupation of a position of trust that makes it wrong for someone to request or accept certain kinds of advantages, irrespective of whether any favour is asked for or provided in return. It ought, the Commission said, to be regarded as bribery in some situations that R's request for, agreement to receive, or acceptance of the advantage is in itself a manifestation of impropriety, irrespective of whether there is a favour sought by P in exchange for the advantage. Two examples provided by the Commission were a senior civil servant accepting a 'thank you' payment, and a trust manager requesting a financial advantage from beneficiaries.

(c) Case 5

3.31   Case 5 is where R requests, agrees to receive, or accepts a financial or other advantage as a <u>reward</u> for the improper performance (whether by R or another person) of a relevant function or activity.

3.32   Again, in this scenario, as with case 4 above, the prosecution does not have to prove that R knew or believed at the time of the request, agreement to receive, or acceptance that the performance of the function or activity was or had been improper.

3.33   In Case 5, the financial or other advantage is a <u>reward</u> for improper performance, ie the bribe takes place after the impropriety has occurred.

(d) Case 6

3.34   Case 6 is where, *in anticipation of <u>or</u> in consequence of* R requesting, agreeing to receive, or accepting a financial or other advantage, a relevant function or activity is performed improperly either by R, or by another person at R's request (on his behalf), or with R's assent or acquiescence.

3.35   It is irrelevant whether R knows or believes that the performance of the function or activity is improper. Furthermore, where a person other than R is performing the function or activity, it is also irrelevant whether that person knows or believes that the performance of the function or activity is improper.

C. DEFINITIONS

1. Relevant Function or Activity

Section 3 defines the scope of a function or activity and the way in which it becomes   3.36
defined as 'relevant' for the purposes of sections 1 and 2. It reflects that which was
established during the lengthy consultation period leading to the Act, namely that
the law of bribery should henceforth apply equally to both public functions and
selected private functions.

The following functions or activities are relevant functions or activities *if,* and   3.37
only if they meet one of the conditions in (A) to (C) at 3.38 below. It is irrelevant
whether the function or activity has no connection with the United Kingdom and
is performed in a country or territory outside of the United Kingdom:[11]

- Any function of a *public nature*—the Act provides no definition of 'public nature',
  it being no doubt contended that this activity will expand and that too restrictive
  a definition would be unhelpful. It is clearly distinguished from an activity connected with a business. However, as if to lay to rest once and for all the distinction
  between public and private bribery, it emphasizes that provided the activity is
  performed in the course of a person's employment or performed by or on behalf
  of a body of persons corporate or unincorporated, it is irrelevant whether the
  function is deemed to be of a public nature or one connected with a business. The
  Explanatory Notes to the Act comment that this is the same phrase that is used in
  the definition of 'public authority' in section 6(3)(b) of the Human Rights Act
  1998, but it is not limited in the same way as in the 1998 Act. The Government
  intends that the Act will apply to Members of Parliament, contending that it is
  'axiomatic that no Peer or Member of Parliament should be above the law'.[12] The
  Law Commission did not believe that it would be desirable to seek to provide a
  comprehensive definition of 'public body', or of 'public function', for the purposes
  of a reformed law of bribery, noting that, to some extent, these notions are shifting
  ones that depend on changes in the way services are provided to the public at local
  and national level.[13]

- Any activity *connected with a business* (including trade or profession).

- Any activity performed *in the course of a person's employment.*

- Any activity performed by or on behalf of a *body of persons* (whether corporate or
  unincorporated).

---

[11] Section 3(6).
[12] *Hansard*, HL, col 1088 (9 December 2009).
[13] Law Commission (n 7 above) para 3.20.

3.38   In relation to activities connected with a business, and those performed in the course of a person's employment, the Explanatory Notes confirm that these two categories straddle the public/private divide.

3.39   These functions or activities must have a special character, by the application of one of the following conditions, in order for them to be 'relevant' functions or activities:

(A) that a person performing the function or activity is expected to perform it in good faith; *and/or*

(B) that a person performing the function or activity is expected to perform it impartially; *and/or*

(C) that a person performing the function or activity is in a position of trust by virtue of performing it.

3.40   The main concern in relation to this provision centres on the terms used, including the apparent vagueness of 'good faith', 'impartiality', and 'trust'. The Law Commission decided against giving these terms a strict legal meaning, having been influenced by representations from the senior judiciary that these should not be linked to their civil law equivalents.[14] During the Committee stage of the Act's passage through the House of Lords, Lord Bach, the Parliamentary-Under-Secretary of State, noted that these terms are 'readily capable of being understood by juries in the relevant context of the case without further elaboration'.[15] The Government has since confirmed that these terms do not require definition, in the hope that this will avoid rigidity, unnecessary complexity, and lacunae in the law.

(a) *Good faith*

3.41   The expectation that someone will act in good faith was at the heart of the Bill presented to Parliament by Transparency International and Hugh Bayley MP. In identifying these three concepts of good faith, impartiality, and trust as being at the heart of the wrong of bribery, the Law Commission sought to provide examples of situations in which an expectation that one will act in good faith might arise:

Example 1
R is P's former tutor, but has now retired from his post. P was not a good student, but needs a glowing reference from R if she is to have any chance of securing a lucrative job. P promises R a large sum of money if R will write such a reference for P. R agrees.

Example 2
The CEO of a major company is asked to assess the merits of taking over a smaller company. Her counterpart at the smaller company is keen that the takeover

---

[14] See the report of the Joint Committee on the Draft Bribery Bill, HC 430-I and HL 115-I (28 July 2009), para 23.

[15] *Hansard*, HL, col GC33 (7 January 2010).

should go ahead. Therefore, the latter offers the CEO of the larger company a substantial payment if she will recommend to her shareholders that the takeover goes ahead. The CEO accepts the offer.

(b) *Impartiality*

Examples envisaged by the Law Commission include third parties employed to   3.42
bring an independent perspective to bear on a dispute, with a view to bringing it to an end, such as a judge or mediator. The Commission recognized that duties of impartiality may arise in other private law contexts. An example it identified was that of a trustee of a discretionary trust required to distribute income on the basis of need as between the beneficiaries.

(c) *Position of trust*

In employing the concept of a 'position of trust' no special reliance is placed on the   3.43
legal concept of trust. The Law Commission opined that a 'position' of trust should not be construed narrowly as if it was a recognized 'relationship' of trust, such as exists between banker and client, doctor and patient, and so forth. People can be in a position of trust in some respect (say, with regard to access to documents or premises) whatever the nature and level of their duties.

Bearing in mind that the Act interprets 'business' as including 'trade or profession', a professional, it might be argued, must always act in good faith, is very often in a position of trust vis-à-vis the client, and may be advising more than one client where impartiality will be assumed. As such, these are clearly functions that could be improperly performed within the meaning of section 3 of the Act.   3.44

The relevant expectations set out above were, in the opinion of the Law   3.45
Commission and Parliament, sufficiently all-encompassing to address the mischief at which the legislation is aimed; for example, it is difficult to imagine a function or activity that can be performed without an expectation that it will be performed in good faith. However, should such circumstances ever arise in the future, the Act will clearly need amending, either to add to the number of conditions in section 3(1)(b) or, as some have suggested, by the removal of these three conditions altogether on the basis that tribunals of fact should have little difficulty in distinguishing that which is proper from that which is improper.

2. Improper Performance

Under section 4, a relevant function or activity: 3.46

(a) is performed improperly if it is performed *in breach of a relevant expectation*; and

(b) is to be treated as being performed improperly if there is a failure to perform the function or activity and that *failure is itself a breach of a relevant expectation*.

A 'relevant expectation'—(a) in relation to a function or activity which meets   3.47
condition (A) or (B) in 3.38 above means the expectation mentioned in the condition

concerned, ie expectations of good faith or impartiality, and (b) in relation to a function or activity which meets condition (C) means any expectation as to the manner in which, or the reasons for which, the function or activity will be performed that arises from the position of trust mentioned in that condition.

3.48   Section 14(3) catches those who, having once held a particular office or role, still carry out their former functions but do so in a manner which would be held to be improper were they still performing their former function or activity.

3.49   The test of what is expected, contained within section 5, is a test of what a 'reasonable person' in the United Kingdom would expect in relation to the performance. In so deciding, where the performance is not subject to the law of any part of the United Kingdom, any local custom or practice is to be disregarded unless it is permitted or required by the written law applicable to the country or territory concerned. 'Written law' means law contained in (a) any written constitution, or provision made by or under legislation, applicable to the country or territory concerned, or (b) any judicial decision which is so applicable and is evidenced in published written sources, ie 'black-letter' law.

3.50   In enacting section 5, Parliament made it clear, as it did in section 6, that past appeals by business to local custom and practice would henceforth be disregarded as unacceptable. Only published written law, which includes legislation, a written constitution, or published judicial decisions permitting the performance or omission in question in unambiguous terms will suffice.

3.51   It must be recognized that in the case of business overseas, a burden is placed on the exporter of goods or services to identify a reliable source for legal advice and then to secure that advice and feel safe in relying upon it. Whatever assistance is given in this regard by the Government's guidance notes, the attention paid to accurately discovering the local written law must colour the discretion of any prosecutor considering possible offences under section 6 or 7. As a number of commentators have pointed out, the requirement to be informed about local law will create a particular burden for small and medium-sized enterprises, without branch offices or large legal services budgets. It does, however, avoid a 'single criminality' approach under which a British juror would apply British standards irrespective of the legal context in which the offence took place.

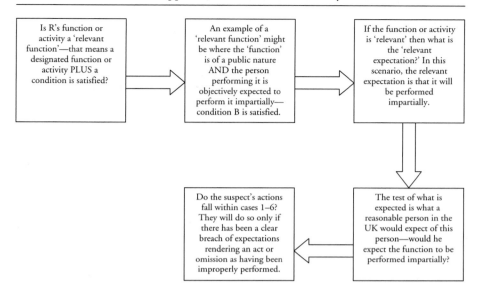

D. ROUTE TO PROSECUTION

The route to any prosecution, whether of a payer or recipient, will be as follows: 3.52

The question for the jury will therefore be whether or not there was an expecta-   3.53
tion that R would act in good faith or impartially, or was in a position of trust, and,
if so, whether R failed to live up to expectations or betrayed the position of trust. In
order to ensure that the provision would be fully understood by businesses and other
affected parties, the Law Commission suggested the following 'lay summary' for the
general bribery offences:

(i) Do not make payments to someone (or favour him in any other way) if you
know that this will involve someone in misuse of his position.

(ii) Do not misuse your position in connection with payments (or other favours) for
yourself or others.[16]

E. TERRITORIAL APPLICATION OF THE 'GENERAL BRIBERY OFFENCES'

Section 12 provides that the offences in section 1, 2, or 6 are committed in any part   3.54
of the United Kingdom if any part of the conduct element takes place in that part
of the United Kingdom.

---

[16] Law Commission (n 7 above) paras 3.78–3.225.

3.55   The effect of section 12(2) to (4) is that, even though all the acts or omissions in question took place abroad, they still constitute the offence if the person performing them is a British national or ordinarily resident[17] in the United Kingdom, a body incorporated in the United Kingdom, or a Scottish partnership.

3.56   Section 12(5) makes it clear that for the purposes of the offence in section 7 (failure of commercial organization to prevent bribery) it is immaterial where the conduct element of the offence occurs.

3.57   Section 12(7) to (9) provides that where proceedings are to be taken in Scotland against a person, such proceedings may be taken in any sheriff court district in which the person is apprehended or in custody, or in such sheriff court district as the Lord Advocate may determine.

3.58   The Serious Fraud Office (SFO), in its evidence to the Joint Committee, said this:

> We welcome the ability to investigate and prosecute companies carrying on part of a business here, irrespective of where they are registered. It is part of creating a world level playing field which would see those companies having to adhere to the same international standards of our own companies and the international community. The SFO will look at appropriate cases with a view to investigation and prosecution. Potential conflicts of jurisdiction will have to be agreed by the respective authorities in each country on an individual case basis. The SFO already has agreements like this with US colleagues.

3.59   Notwithstanding that the relevant provisions of the Anti-Terrorism Crime and Security Act 2001 were designed to bring the United Kingdom into line with the OECD Convention,[18] critics continued to doubt whether the United Kingdom was really able to deal effectively with the bribery of foreign public officials, particularly where the bribers took pains to do little or nothing in furtherance of the crime in the United Kingdom. Under section 12 of the 2010 Act, these doubts are now removed.

F. GENERAL BRIBERY OFFENCES BY BODIES CORPORATE

3.60   Section 14 is aimed at individuals who consent to or connive at bribery committed by a body corporate (of any kind) or Scottish partnership. It *does not* apply to the corporate offence of failure to prevent bribery in section 7, and the Government has confirmed that there is no possibility of individual liability ever arising under section 14 in the event of the commission of a section 7 offence.[19]

3.61   In the first instance, it must be established that the body corporate or Scottish partnership has indeed been guilty of an offence under section 1, 2, or 6. That established,

---

[17] See n 17 below for discussion of the meaning of 'ordinarily resident'. This section ensures that individuals cannot live within the United Kingdom without being subject to the same criminal law as its citizens.

[18] Ibid.

[19] Letter from Parliamentary-Under-Secretary of State, Claire Ward, to Jonathan Djanogly MP, 29 March 2009, available at <http://www.parliament.uk/deposits/depositedpapers/2010/DEP2010-0974.pdf> (last visited 6 July 2010).

section 14 provides that a 'senior officer' of a body corporate or Scottish partnership, or a person purporting to act in such a capacity, is guilty of the *same offence* if he has 'consented to' or 'connived in' the commission of the offence. Proof of neglect will not suffice in establishing individual criminal liability; only proof of 'consent or connivance' will do. The consent and connivance doctrine makes senior officers liable only for the offence committed by the company, not for an offence committed by individual employees.

It should be noted that in this situation the body corporate and the senior officer are *both* guilty of the main bribery offence. Section 14 does not create a separate offence of 'consent or connivance'.   3.62

Section 14(3) makes clear that for a 'senior officer' or similar person to be guilty he must have a close connection to the United Kingdom, as defined in section 12(4).   3.63

1. Senior Officer

Under section 14(4) a 'senior officer' means: 3.64

(a) in relation to a body corporate, a director, manager, secretary, or other similar officer of the body corporate, and

(b) in relation to a Scottish partnership, a partner in the partnership.

A 'director', in relation to a body corporate whose affairs are managed by its members, means a member of the body corporate.   3.65

2. Close Connection with the United Kingdom

Under section 12(4) a person has a close connection with the United Kingdom if, and only if, the person was one of the following at the time the acts or omissions concerned were done or made: 3.66

(c) a British citizen;

(d) a British overseas territories citizen;

(e) a British national (overseas);

(f) a British overseas citizen;

(g) a person who, under the British Nationality Act 1981, was a British subject;

(h) a British protected person within the meaning of that Act;[20]

(i) an individual ordinarily resident in the United Kingdom;[21]

---

[20] 'British protected person' means a person who is a member of any class of person declared to be British protected persons by an Order in Council for the time being in force under s 38 or who is a British protected person by virtue of the Solomon Islands Act 1978.

[21] *Halsbury's Laws of England* provides the following broad assistance on the meaning of 'ordinarily resident': '"Ordinary residence" refers to a person's abode in a particular place or country which he has adopted voluntarily and for settled (but not indefinite) purposes as part of the regular order of his life for the time being

(j) a body incorporated under the law of any part of the United Kingdom;

(k) a Scottish partnership.

3. Consent and Connivance

3.67 Consent and connivance provisions are commonplace in regulatory statutes, such as those dealing with health and safety. The meaning of 'consent or connive' has been shown to be flexible. The Law Commission has previously likened the terms to those of encouragement or tolerance. In its broadest consideration of these terms, carried out ahead of a lengthy consultation period on reform of the law of bribery, the Law Commission said this of the concept of connivance:

> it is wider than that provided for by the doctrine of complicity. First, in theory it is possible for someone to 'connive' at the commission of an offence (to know it may occur but to do nothing to prevent its commission) without providing actual assistance or encouragement. Secondly, connivance may occur through reckless conduct (knowing that there is a risk of offending but doing nothing) whereas, speaking in very broad terms, complicity requires intention or knowledge as to the offending behaviour.'

3.68 The Law Commission goes on to assert that 'connivance at the culpable actions of the corporate perpetrator may be reckless on the part of a high-ranking member of an organisation, as well as intentional or knowing'.[22]

3.69 'Consent' would certainly suggest the involvement of active knowledge and agreement on the part of the senior officer.

3.70 Commenting on a similar provision in the Health and Safety at Work Act 1974, Lord Hope, in *R v Chargot*[23] commented that: '[N]o fixed rule can be laid down as to what the prosecution must identify and prove in order to establish that the officer's state of mind was such as to amount to consent, connivance or neglect'.

(whether of short or long duration).' Practitioners should refer to *Halsbury's Laws of England*, 5th edn, last updated 14 May 2010 (editor-in-chief, Lord Mackay of Clashfern), and in particular to para 134 of Vol 4(2), *British Nationality, Immigration and Asylum*, for a full consideration of the relevant authorities on the meaning of 'ordinarily resident'. The Law Commission also considered the meaning of the phrase in its final report (n 7 above) (from para 8.34), and practitioners are urged to refer to that document for additional guidance. The Commission cites therein the following passage from Dicey, Morris, and Collins, *The Conflict of Laws* (14th edn, 2006), in which the following definition of ordinary residence is proffered: 'It has sometimes been said that "ordinary residence" means nothing more or less than "residence", but it is submitted that the better view is that the adjective does add something, an element of continuity, order, or settled purpose'. The use of this phrase ensures consistency of approach with the 2001 Act. The Law Commission also noted the discussion of the meaning of the term during the passage of the International Criminal Court Bill through Parliament, at which time Lord Goodhart said that, by way of contrast with its use in tax legislation, 'the residence test will be applied for the purpose of founding jurisdiction over criminal offences. In those circumstances, the court is likely to interpret the residence test strictly': HL, col 421 (8 March 2001).

[22] Law Commission (n 1 above) paras 9.21–9.37.
[23] [2008] UKHL 73, [2009] 1 WLR 1 at [33].

4. Fraud Act 2006 and Theft Act 1968

The consent or connivance provision deliberately follows the model of section 12 of 3.71
the Fraud Act 2006 and, previously, section 18 of the Theft Act 1968, among others.
The Law Commission report[24] noted that: 'there is a compelling case to extend the
"consent and connivance" regime applicable in fraud cases to bribery offences'. In
his memorandum to the Joint Committee,[25] the Director of Public Prosecutions
said:

> The offence of 'consent or connivance' to the general offences or of bribing a foreign public official
> will be unused until there is a likelihood of prosecutions of corporations for the underlying
> offences. There would appear to have been no prosecutions by the CPS under the equivalent
> provisions in section 18 Theft Act 1968 and section 12 Fraud Act 2006.

Since the time of that memorandum, the company Innospec has been success- 3.72
fully prosecuted for an offence of foreign bribery under section 1 of the Prevention
of Corruption Act 1906, as amended.

Practitioners will also recall similar provisions, absent any requirement for neglect, 3.73
in section 28 of the Public Order Act 1986, section 72 of the Competition Act
1998, section 18 of the Terrorism Act 2006, and section 110 of the Copyright,
Designs and Patents Act 1988.

---

[24] Law Commission (n 7 above) para 6.132.
[25] Memorandum submitted by the Director of Public Prosecutions (BB 16), June 2009.

4
BRIBERY OF FOREIGN
PUBLIC OFFICIALS

A. THE UK'S INTERNATIONAL OBLIGATIONS UNDER THE OECD CONVENTION

The United Kingdom is a party to a number of international instruments concerned   4.01
with bribery and corruption. That which has most significantly shaped the Act is
the OECD Convention on Combating Bribery of Foreign Public Officials in
International Business Transactions ('the Convention'), which entered into force on
15 February 1999.

Article 1.1 of the Convention requires: 4.02

a. each Party [to] take such measures as may be necessary to establish that it is a criminal offence
under its law for any person intentionally to offer, promise or give any undue pecuniary or
other advantage, whether directly or through intermediaries to a foreign public official, for that
official or for a third party, in order that the official act or refrain from acting in relation to the
performance of official duties, in order to obtain or retain business or other improper advantage
in the conduct of international business.

The UK's first attempt to meet its international obligations under the Convention   4.03
was the amendment of the existing statutory and common law offences of corruption
by Part 12 of the Anti-Terrorism, Crime and Security Act 2001. Part 12, which came
into force on 14 February 2002, extended the territorial application of the law in two
respects. Following the amendment, it was irrelevant that the recipient of the bribe
(and in the case of the 1906 Act, his principal) was outside of, or had no connection

to, the United Kingdom.[1] It also extended the scope of the law to encompass acts of bribery committed abroad by UK nationals or bodies incorporated under UK law, provided the acts would constitute an offence had they taken place here.[2] It should be noted that the Convention did not require this extra-territorial jurisdiction to extend to foreign nationals ordinarily resident in the United Kingdom, or to foreign regis-tered companies doing business in the United Kingdom.[3]

4.04   When considering the initial response to the Convention, it should be noted that the Law Commission's previous report[4] was consequently subject to consultation. It was therefore anticipated that the amendments made by the 2001 Act would be no more than a temporary measure. That was not to be the case. The OECD's Working Group on Bribery in International Business Transactions ('the Working Group') acknowledged in March 2003 the 'very significant steps' taken by the United Kingdom but recommended the enactment of a comprehensive statute to clarify the law, given a number of 'areas of uncertainty'. These criticisms did not wholly and exclusively relate to the requirements of the Convention to criminalize bribery of foreign public officials in business transactions, but rather to the whole of the United Kingdom's anti-corruption law. This was not surprising given that the United Kingdom's general anti-corruption laws were modified in an attempt to comply with the Convention.

4.05   Areas of uncertainty included the continued focus on the agent/principal rela-tionship, which could lead to interpretations that were not compliant with the Convention, uncertainty within and inconsistency between definitions of key ele-ments of the existing offences, and the absolute prohibition on allowing consider-ations of international relations or economic interest to influence the investigation or prosecution of bribery of foreign public officials. It was this latter concern that came to a head in the controversial decision by the Serious Fraud Office (SFO) in December 2006 to discontinue the prosecution of BAE Systems for alleged bribes paid in connection with the sale of aircraft to Saudi Arabia.[5]

4.06   Given the failure to remedy the identified deficiencies, the Working Group was moved in 2005 to put pressure on the United Kingdom in its Phase 2 Report, rec-ommending that the United Kingdom 'enact at the earliest possible date compre-hensive legislation whose scope clearly includes the bribery of a foreign public official'.[6] It took a further five years to enact legislation, albeit legislation which is arguably the most stringent among all the Convention signatories.

4.07   Although the Convention did not specifically require the implementation of a separate offence covering only the bribery of foreign public officials[7], the Act

[1] Anti-Terrorism, Crime and Security Act 2001, s 108.
[2] Ibid, s 109.
[3] Bribery Act 2010, s 12.
[4] Law Commission, *Legislating the Criminal Code: Corruption* (Law Com No 248, 1998).
[5] *R (Corner House Research and others) v Director of the Serious Fraud Office* [2008] UKHL 60.
[6] Working Group, *United Kingdom: Phase 2 Report on the Application of the Convention on Combating Bribery of Foreign Public Officials in International Business Transactions and the 1997 Recommendation on Combating Bribery in International Business Transactions* (March 2005) para 248.
[7] See para 3 of the Commentaries to the Convention.

contains an offence deliberately drafted to reflect the broad language and principle used in the Convention. The Law Commission was of the view that this would demonstrate the United Kingdom's commitment to its international obligations. The Joint Parliamentary Committee, in its report on the draft Bill, said that this 'represents an important step in putting the United Kingdom's compliance with its international obligations beyond doubt, particularly those owed to the [OECD]'.[8] During the House of Lords debate on the draft Bill, Lord Bach, on behalf of the Government, said that the use of a 'bespoke offence would further underline this country's commitment to international efforts to stamp out the particularly insidious practice of bribing foreign public officials'.[9]

There was also a desire to ring fence the interpretation of the general bribery   4.08 offence. According to the general principles of statutory construction, domestic legislation designed to enforce an obligation under an international treaty is to be construed as being 'intended to carry out the obligation and not to be inconsistent with it'.[10] Given the evolving nature of any convention, and particularly the OECD Convention keeping pace, as it must, with developments in international commerce and the changing threat of corruption, it was clearly desirable to have a separate offence of bribing a foreign public official. The separate offence means that courts need not be concerned with the possible consequential effects in a wholly domestic context of interpreting the general offence in accordance with the Convention.

A further advantage is that such construction is more straightforward if the sig-   4.09 nificant language in the one mirrored that in the other. As the Law Commission noted,[11] the appellate courts' opportunity to interpret key provisions in the Act is likely to be limited, so the use of language adopted by other parties to the Convention may allow the use of comparative jurisprudence in order to understand the scope of the offence. For example, the words 'obtaining or retaining business' are to be found in the US Foreign and Corrupt Practices Act 1977, the New Zealand Crimes Act 1961, and the Australian Criminal Code Act 1995, while very similar language is used by Canada in its Corruption of Foreign Public Officials Act 1998.

B. OVERVIEW OF THE OFFENCE

Section 6 of the Bribery Act 2010 criminalizes the act of bribing a foreign public   4.10 official where the payer intends to influence the official in his capacity as such an official. There is no corresponding offence for the official himself. The Convention does not require the conduct of the foreign official to be criminalized by the signatory

---

[8] See Report of the Joint Committee, on the Draft Bribery Bill (28 July 2009) (HC 430-I and HL 115-I) para 64.

[9] *Hansard*, HL, col 1087 (9 December 2009).

[10] *Garland v British Rail* [1983] 2 AC 751, 771, per Lord Diplock.

[11] See Law Commission, *Reforming Bribery* (Law Com No 313, 2008) para 5.67.

states: rather it has as its focus the active bribery committed by the payer of the bribe.

4.11 Even if a corresponding offence for the official's conduct were to exist it is unlikely in practice that prosecutors in England and Wales would be in a position to prosecute such an offence, unless of course they were able to intercept and charge the official in question in the United Kingdom, or in Europe where a European arrest warrant (EAW) could be issued. Although some submissions to the Law Commission were in favour of the extension of the offence, the main arguments against adoption of this course were the undesirability of criminalizing here behaviour that was not criminal in the official's home jurisdiction, and the risk that other states, including those whose trials failed to meet basic standards of fairness, would feel entitled similarly to extend their own laws.

4.12 The conduct and mental elements of the offence are examined in detail below. It will be seen that, unlike the general bribery offence under section 1, there is no requirement to prove an intention to induce or reward improper performance on the part of the foreign public official. The jury is not called upon to analyse whether the actions of the bribed official would, if they were carried out as the payer of the bribe wished, constitute a breach of that official's duty. It is enough simply to prove an intention on the part of the payer of the bribe to influence the official by conferring any advantage which is not specifically permitted by the written law. As Lord Tunnicliffe said during the passage of the Bill through the House of Lords, the 'offence is formulated so as to avoid the need to identify precisely the nature of the functions of and duty owed by foreign public officials. Such matters have proved to be one of the difficulties experienced by prosecutors in this kind of case under the current law'.[12]

4.13 That said, there is a clear and intentional overlap between this offence and the general bribery offence under section 1. In some instances of bribes paid to foreign public officials there will be evidence of improper performance such that either charge could, in theory, be proffered.

4.14 Although the offence contains a number of complicated elements and alternatives, the Law Commission suggested a rule of thumb to guide behaviour: 'Do not intentionally give advantages to foreign public officials, to gain or retain business, without a legal justification'.[13]

C. THE CONDUCT ELEMENT

4.15 In section 6 of the Act, the briber is denoted as 'P' and the foreign public official as 'F'. The conduct element of the offence is the direct or indirect offer, promise, or gift by P of any financial or other advantage to F or another.[14]

---

[12] *Hansard*, HL, col GC41 (7 January 2010).
[13] Law Commission (n 10 above) para 5.76.
[14] Section 6(3)(a).

Like the general bribery offences the offence is defined in the inchoate mode. It is 4.16
sufficient for P to offer or promise an advantage. It does not have to accrue to F or,
as discussed below, his nominee.

By including indirect offers the Act covers instances where the bribe is offered, 4.17
promised, or paid via an intermediary. Such intermediaries will include the obvious
categories of those affiliated to P, such as sales representatives, consultants, or foreign
subsidiaries, but also those who might be affiliated to F, such as foreign political parties or party officials who themselves are not foreign public officials.

The offence is also committed in cases of indirect benefit—where F nominates 4.18
another person to receive the advantage, or assents or acquiesces to that other person
receiving it.[15] The Law Commission was of the view[16] that this goes beyond the
requirements of the Convention, which covers advantages provided 'to a foreign
public official, for that official or for a third party'. The Law Commission considered that this passage encompassed the receipt by F of an advantage for a third party,
but not necessarily where F asked for the advantage to accrue directly to a third
party. This omission was seen as unjustifiable.

The identity of the other person and his relationship to F are, in terms of the 4.19
offence itself, irrelevant. However, as a matter of evidence, the fact that F's spouse,
business partner, or a company in which F has an interest, receives a financial or
other advantage from P may well be compelling.

The Law Commission considered a number of situations where the Convention 4.20
did not require the law to trespass. These included the provision of an advantage to
a person connected to F but where F neither requests nor acquiesces to it[17] and the
provision of an advantage to a third party who would seek to use his influence to
obtain or retain business.[18] The former was rejected on the basis that there may be
nothing 'undue' about the receipt. The latter was not without controversy, but was
consistent with the UK Government having opted out of Article 12 of the EU
Criminal Law Convention on Corruption,[19] the fear being that it might encompass
legitimate lobbying activities.

The meaning of 'financial or other advantage', which also occurs in the general 4.21
bribery offence, is to be determined as a matter of common sense by the jury.[20] The
issue of corporate hospitality and promotional expenses are dealt with elsewhere and
section 9 guidance is awaited.

In addition the prosecutor must prove that F is neither permitted nor required by 4.22
the written law applicable to him to be influenced in his capacity as a foreign public
official by the offer, promise, or gift. We examine the concept of influencing the

---

[15] Section 6(3)(a)(ii).
[16] Law Commission (n 10 above) para 5.40.
[17] Ibid para 5.40.
[18] So-called 'pure trade in influence': see Law Commission (ibid) paras 5.43 *et seq.*
[19] Which covers the promising, giving, or offering, directly or indirectly, of any undue advantage to anyone
who asserts or confirms that he is able to exert an improper influence over the decision-making of any person
referred to (in relation to the principal offence).
[20] Bribery Bill Explanatory Notes, para 15.

foreign public official in his capacity as such and the question of the applicable written law below.

D. THE MENTAL ELEMENT

4.23   There are two separate and distinct mental elements to the offence.

4.24   First, P must intend to influence F in his capacity as a foreign public official.[21] This means influencing F in the performance of his functions as such an official, including an omission to exercise those functions. It also includes any use (or abuse) of F's position as such an official even if it is not within his lawful authority.[22]

4.25   The Act adopts the language of the Convention, which requires intention rather than recklessness. While a payment to an agent, part of which was to be passed on to 'such [foreign public official] as has the power to award the contract', are included within the scope of the offence, situations where there is no more than a foreseeable risk of influencing a foreign public official by the offer of an advantage are not.[23] It will be for the jury to determine by reference to the evidence whether a defendant who professes to have left the matter to the agent, and so did not form such an intention, is telling the truth.

4.26   The Law Commission's rationale for this approach, carried through into the Act, was the potential unfairness of criminal liability based on foreseeable risk, where the risk (that a foreign public official might be influenced in his official capacity) was inherently difficult to assess. This is to be contrasted with offences for which recklessness is sufficient *mens rea*, such as criminal damage and manslaughter, where the consequences of one's actions are likely to be easier to assess.[24]

4.27   The second limb of the definition of influencing F in F's capacity as a foreign public official ('any use of F's position as such an official, even if not within F's authority') suggests that P need not know (or perhaps care) what F's actual functions are in order to form the necessary intention. There may be an argument that the words limit the offence to bribes paid to influence the functions possessed by the type of foreign public official to whom the bribe is paid.

4.28   The second mental element is that P must intend to bribe in order to obtain or retain business or an advantage in the conduct of business.[25] The Act confirms that the expression 'business' includes a trade or profession, but it does not specify that the 'business' or 'advantage in business' which P intends to obtain or retain must be connected to him. It is not a necessary ingredient of the offence. That said, in demonstrating that P had the requisite intention, it is plain that a contract awarded to P's employer or his principal is evidentially significant.

---

[21] Section 6(1).
[22] Section 6(4).
[23] Law Commission (n 10 above) para 5.77.
[24] Ibid paras 5.112 *et seq*.
[25] Section 6(2).

E. FOREIGN PUBLIC OFFICIAL

The definition of 'foreign public official' is, by design, an autonomous definition, 4.29 and not dependent upon local legal principles. Again, it reflects the requirements of the Convention. The definition is widely drawn to include the direct agents of the state, ie those holding a legislative, administrative, or judicial position[26] or who exercise a public function for or on behalf of a foreign country, as well as those who exercise public functions on behalf of public agencies and enterprises in foreign countries.[27] The latter category clearly includes state-owned businesses, although the extent to which any given individual exercises a public function for that body will be a question of fact for the jury.

Also included within the category of foreign public officials are officials and agents 4.30 of public international organizations[28], ie whose members are countries, governments, or other public international organizations.[29]

Neither foreign political parties nor party officials are included within the defini- 4.31 tion. Payments to such parties are not covered by the Act, except, of course, where they are improperly used as intermediaries to pass on an advantage to a foreign public official, or are nominated to receive such benefit by a foreign public official. While in one-party states in particular this may seem to be an unjustified omission, the practical difficulties in determining who may or may not be perfectly entitled to accept advantages and who is or is not a member of the political party were seen as insurmountable.

In addition, prospective foreign public officials are not covered by the definition 4.32 of foreign public official. It may be that both the payment and receipt of bribes by and to such individuals would fall within the scope of the general bribery offences.

1. Advantage Neither Permitted Nor Required

At the core of the Convention is the concept of a bribe being 'any undue pecuniary 4.33 or other advantage'. While the key word 'undue' is undefined, the Commentaries to the Convention provide (at paragraphs 7 and 8) that:

7. It is also an offence irrespective of, inter alia, the value of the advantage, its results, perceptions of local custom, the tolerance of such payments by local authorities, or the alleged necessity of the payment in order to obtain or retain business or other improper advantage.
8. It is not an offence, however, if the advantage was permitted or required by the written law or regulation of the foreign public official's country, including case law.

With the Convention firmly in mind, the Act provides that for an advantage to 4.34 be legitimately given to a foreign public official he must be either permitted or

---

[26] Section 6(5)(b)(i).
[27] Section 6(5)(b)(ii).
[28] Section 6(5)(c).
[29] Section 6(6).

required by written law to be influenced by it in his capacity as a foreign public official. The Government was adamant that no account should be taken of custom or practice, and that the applicable law should be written law, as defined within the Act.[30] The aim was clearly to restrict the circumstances in which advantages could legitimately be provided to foreign public officials.

4.35   The written law which applies depends on the foreign public official, and the categories are described at section 6(7):

(i)   where the functions intended to be influenced would be subject to the law of any part of the United Kingdom, then the law of that part of the United Kingdom;[31]

(ii) where (i) does not apply, but the official is an agent of a public international agent, then the written rules of that organization;[32]

(iii) where (i) and (ii) do not apply, the law of the foreign public official's country so far as is contained in a written constitution, legislative provision, or written judicial decision.[33]

2. Reasonable Belief Not a Defence

4.36   Key to whether the provision of an advantage comes within the definition of a bribe is whether it was permitted by written law. The Law Commission contemplated a statutory defence of mistaken but reasonable belief in the legitimate nature of a payment to a foreign public official. It was envisaged that such a defence would take into account local legal advice received. Those in support of such a defence noted that mistake in English law can, in limited circumstances, operate as a defence.

4.37   However, in the face of strong objections from, among others, the OECD, this provision did not make it through to the Government's draft Bill or Act. In the House of Lords, Lord Tunnicliffe, on behalf of the Government, said:

ignorance of the local law will not be a defence in relation to the offence in the Bill. Those involved in international business activities should have ready access to legal advice on the legitimacy of

---

[30] See, eg Lord Tunnicliffe, *Hansard*, HL col 126 (2 February 2010): 'The offence is . . . drafted so as to prevent all but the written law of the state concerned from being a relevant consideration as regards the legitimacy of the payment. The reasons for this are twofold. First, we wish to avoid local custom and practice being a relevant consideration. If our Bill is to make an effective contribution to the efforts at the national and international level to encourage the developing world to abandon the culture of toleration of bribery we need to provide a robust deterrent. This offence is designed to fulfil that need by, among other things, preventing local customs and practice from being prayed in aid as a defence. Secondly, and extremely importantly, the experience of prosecutors working with the current law is that it is extremely difficult to pinpoint with sufficient certainty what duties or expectations apply to any individual foreign public official. Local circumstances vary immensely'.

[31] Section 6(7)(a).

[32] Section 6(7)(b).

[33] Section 6(7)(c).

payments to foreign officials and should think twice before offering, promising or giving advantages to foreign officials.[34]

In the House of Commons the Government reiterated that: 4.38

the offence is intended to send a powerful message that those involved in international business should think twice before offering, promising or giving payments or other advantages to foreign public officials. The introduction of a reasonable belief defence would detract from that powerful message and undermine the policy aims of the offence to combat foreign bribery.[35]

On one view the absence of the defence may lead to an unintended consequence. 4.39 Where an employee confers an advantage on a foreign public official, relying on legal advice obtained by his employer that the same was permissible, he cannot rely on a defence of reasonable belief if the advice is shown to be erroneous. However, the employing company, for whose benefit the advantage was conferred, may be able to raise the statutory defence of adequate procedures to a charge of failing to prevent bribery. The company would seek to argue that its procedures, including taking and following local legal advice, were adequate to prevent bribery.

Although in these circumstances a sensible application of prosecutorial discretion 4.40 can be anticipated, in the event of prosecution of the employer for failing to prevent bribery offence the courts will look at all the circumstances, rather than checking whether the 'legal advice' box has been ticked. Procedures designed to satisfy the statutory defence under section 7 must apply both to the general bribery offence under section 1 and the section 6 offence. The procedures must be adequate to prevent bribery of either type. Reliance on local legal advice alone will not be enough.

---

[34] *Hansard*, HL, col GC2 (7 January 2010).
[35] *Hansard*, HL, col 43 (16 March 2010).

5

FAILURE OF COMMERCIAL ORGANIZATIONS TO PREVENT BRIBERY

A. OVERVIEW

Section 7 of the Act creates a wholly new offence applicable to a 'relevant commercial organisation' ('the organization'). The offence is committed when a person associated with the organization bribes another intending either to obtain or retain business for that organization or intending to obtain or retain a business advantage for that organization.   5.01

This is a strict liability offence, with a defence available if the organization can prove that it had in place adequate procedures designed to prevent the briber from undertaking such conduct.   5.02

Before examining this novel offence it may be of assistance to look briefly at the reasoning behind its creation.   5.03

The Law Commission, upon whose draft Bill the Act is substantially based, gave the following justification for criminalizing the failure by companies and partnerships to prevent bribery on their behalf. The Commission believed that business entities were in the best position to ensure that the enormous damage done by the toleration of bribery—especially in relation to overseas trade—was reduced or even eliminated worldwide. It recognized that the present state of English law made it difficult to bring either criminal or civil proceedings effectively against entities that appeared to be prepared to allow bribes to be employed as a means of establishing or enhancing their trading positions. The Law Commission considered, and Parliament agreed, albeit by choosing a regulatory model rather than one based on negligence, that it was essential to ensure that a high ethical standard was enforced for all business entities. Thus, unfair competition would be avoided and the law would punish   5.04

bad actors regardless of whether actionable financial loss could be proven. Furthermore, by this enactment Parliament would be complying with the letter and the spirit of the United Kingdom's international obligations by deterring and punishing business entities indifferent to the commission of bribery on their behalf.

5.05 Because reform of the United Kingdom's law on corporate criminal liability is some way off, and because of widespread concern about the Law Commission's original proposal based on negligence as a way of avoiding the pitfalls of the attribution principle currently used to determine such liability, an offence of strict liability was chosen. In so doing, Parliament recognized that 'in a world where corporate decision making may be highly decentralised, and may take place in a multi-national context'[1] the identification doctrine based on the need to discover a directing mind representing the corporate mind and will, was entirely inadequate.

5.06 Although it is not anticipated that this new offence or that in section 6 of the Act will lead to a significant increase in the number of prosecutions, Parliament appears to have accepted the view that it would henceforth be easier for prosecutors to pursue businesses that in effect perpetuate the culture and practice of bribery. In particular it had in mind businesses that operate without safeguards to promote high standards of integrity, in industries, regions, or countries vulnerable to the lure of malpractice.[2]

5.07 Although critics of this provision during its passage through Parliament accused the Government of 'gold-plating' the United Kingdom's international obligations, this criticism was rejected, and the United Kingdom may thus move from being a country characterized as ignoring its obligations under international instruments, to one possibly establishing a new 'gold standard' for ethical business practices.

5.08 The offence under section 7 is only committed if an associated person, defined in section 8, is proven, to a criminal standard of proof, to have committed an offence of bribery as defined in section 1 or 6 regardless of whether that person was prosecuted for the offence, and provided the bribery was for the purposes of section 7(1) (a) or (b), ie for the intended business benefits of the defendant entity. This takes account of the reality that an agent living overseas may never be prosecuted at all.

B. THE OFFENCE

1. Relevant Commercial Organization

5.09 The offence can only be committed by a relevant commercial organization[3]—a group that comprises companies and partnerships with the requisite connection to the United Kingdom. This connection is present if the organization is either formed (in the case of partnerships) or incorporated (in the case of bodies corporate) under

---

[1] Law Commission, *Reforming Bribery* (Law Com No 313, 2008) para 6.27.
[2] Ibid para 6.60.
[3] Section 7(1) and (5).

the law of any part of the United Kingdom, or is an organization formed or incorporated overseas but which carries on a business or part of its business in any part of the United Kingdom.[4]

As the Act defines partnerships by reference to the statutory provisions under which they are formed, in order to cover overseas partnerships doing business in the United Kingdom the Act extends the definition to include firms of a similar character formed under the laws of a foreign jurisdiction.[5] Proceedings against a partnership are taken in the name of the partnership rather than the names of the partners.[6]   5.10

To come within the definition of a relevant commercial organization the defendant company or partnership (referred to hereafter as 'the corporate') must carry on a business.[7]   5.11

2. The Bribe

The prosecutor must prove the commission of an offence of bribing another person (an offence under section 1) or an offence of bribing a foreign public official (an offence under section 6).[8] However, it is not necessary for anyone to be prosecuted for the underlying bribery offence, let alone convicted. Indeed, the corporate can be prosecuted for the failure to prevent the offence even where the bribe payer cannot be prosecuted in the United Kingdom. The Act criminalizes bribery offences where any act or omission which forms part of the offence takes place in the United Kingdom, or where no such act or omission takes place in the United Kingdom but the accused has a close connection with the United Kingdom.[9] However, for the purposes of the offence under section 7 there is no requirement for the bribe to have been paid by someone with a close connection to the United Kingdom or for any act or omission forming part of the offence to take place in the United Kingdom.[10]   5.12

In addition to proving that the underlying bribery offence took place, the prosecutor must also prove that the person who paid the bribe: 5.13

• was a person associated with the corporate; and

• intended to obtain or retain business for the corporate, or obtain or retain an advantage in the conduct of the business of the corporate.

These elements are considered below.   5.14

---

[4] Section 7(5).
[5] Section 7(5).
[6] Section 15(1).
[7] Which includes a trade or profession—s 7(5).
[8] Section 7(3)(a).
[9] Section 12(2) and (3).
[10] Section 7(3)(b) and s 12(5).

3. Associated Person

5.15   Section 8 defines an associated person. The essential feature of the relationship which determines whether the payer of the bribe is associated with the corporate is the performance of services, other than the bribe under consideration, by the former for or on behalf of the latter.[11]

5.16   The capacity in which the services are performed is immaterial,[12] although the Act identifies three relationships in which such services might be performed: employee, agent, and subsidiary.[13] However, it is clear that these are examples only, and the issue is not to be determined solely by reference to the nature of the relationship. The question of whether the payer of the bribe performs services on behalf of the corporate is determined by reference to all the relevant circumstances.[14] There is, however, a rebuttable presumption that an associated person who is an employee of the defendant business performs services on behalf of his employer.

5.17   It is understood that the issue of a parent company's liability for a subsidiary is one of the issues due to be considered as part of the Law Commission's review of corporate criminal liability. Under the Act it is a question of fact in each case, considering all the relevant circumstances, whether a subsidiary or joint venture which paid a bribe performed services for or on behalf of the corporate. This is likely to include the extent to which the corporate had control over the person or entity paying the bribes.

4. Intention to Obtain or Retain Business etc

5.18   Although, insofar as the corporate is concerned, the offence is one of strict liability, the intention of the payer of the bribe is relevant and must be proved.

5.19   The prosecutor must demonstrate that the bribe was paid with the intention of obtaining or retaining business for the corporate or obtaining or retaining an advantage in the conduct of business for the corporate.

5.20   Although the offence of bribery of foreign public officials requires proof of a similar intention—albeit without reference to the business of the corporate[15]—this is an additional element to be proved where the alleged bribery offence which the corporate failed to prevent was an offence under section 1. Of course, where a bribe is paid and results in the award of business to the corporate, a jury is unlikely to accept that this was an unintended consequence.

5.21   It should be noted that this section, together with section 8, makes clear, in contrast to section 12 of the Act, that there is no need for the associated person to have a close connection to the United Kingdom. Provided the undertaking falls within

---

[11] Section 8(1).
[12] Section 8(2).
[13] Section 8(3).
[14] Section 8(4).
[15] Section 6(2).

the definition of a 'relevant commercial organisation' as defined by section 7(5) that should be enough to found jurisdiction in the UK courts.

5. Adequate Procedures

Although the offence is one of strict liability, or, perhaps more accurately, vicarious liability based upon the actions of an associated person, the Act provides a defence for the corporate to prove, on a balance of probabilities, that it had in place adequate procedures designed to prevent associated persons from paying bribes. The defence is available notwithstanding the commission of an offence of bribery which the procedures failed to prevent.   5.22

There was much debate during the legislative process about what sort of procedures might be regarded as adequate. Initially, the Government's response was that it was very difficult to be prescriptive, making it clear that there was no 'one size fits all' solution. However, during the latter stages of the Bill's progress through Parliament, an additional clause was introduced, obliging the Secretary of State to publish guidance about procedures that those potentially caught by the new offence can put in place.[16] Such guidance can be revised from time to time in whole or in part.[17]   5.23

The Government has stated that such guidance will be generic only, and not prescriptive.   5.24

The Government has promised that guidance will not seek to micromanage the policy of business entities or involve them in excess expenditure. The guidance will be updated from time to time. The Government has also undertaken that adequate procedures will be interpreted in the guidance in a flexible and proportionate way and take into account the size of the corporate and the risks associated with the business sector in which it operates.   5.25

While the exact text of the guidance is awaited at the time of publication of this book, it is anticipated that it will be produced at least three months before the date of implementation, which initially appeared to suggest that it would be published in late June or early July 2010. Following a change in Government and attendant delays flowing from that, more recent forecasts predict a delay in publication until 2011.   5.26

From what has been said publicly by the Government it is envisaged that the guidance will encompass the following areas: 5.27

(a) commitment at the highest level of an organization;

(b) risk assessment and management;

(c) clear and transparent policies and procedures;

(d) effective implementation that goes beyond paper compliance;

---

[16] Section 9(1).
[17] Section 9(2).

(e) effective due diligence of business relationships and open accurate reporting;

(f) monitoring and review.

5.28   It is anticipated that the guidance will also refer to:

(a) facilitation payments;

(b) corporate hospitality;

(c) agents, intermediaries, and joint ventures or syndicates to the extent that they relate to the procedures put in place by commercial organizations to prevent bribery.

5.29   The Government has emphazised throughout the passage of the legislation that the guidance is not intended to provide a box-ticking exercise for commercial enterprises. Whether or not procedures are adequate to satisfy the requirements of the adequate procedures defence will be a matter for the courts to decide having regard to all the relevant circumstances. It will not be a matter of surprise to the reader that Lord Henley, upon the second reading of the Bribery Bill, raised the following probing queries:

• Who is to judge what is adequate and what is not?
• If a company has stringent rules in place, checks on its employees, has transparent accounting and so on, but a determined associate of that company still manages to bribe another, were those procedures adequate? They did not, after all, prevent the offence of bribery taking place.
• What about a company with weak procedures in place which nevertheless managed, perhaps more by chance than anything else, to stop an embryonic plan to commit bribery? Which of those cases should be prosecuted?
• What about the commercial organisations themselves? How will they know if they have put in place adequate procedures?

5.30   Those tasked with advising companies on the meaning of 'adequate procedures' may themselves gain some insight by a review of US sentencing guidelines, under which the following elements are considered vital to a comprehensive compliance programme:

(1) due diligence to prevent and detect criminal conduct;

(2) promoting a culture that encourages ethical conduct and a commitment to compliance with the law;

(3) establishing standards and procedures to prevent and detect criminal conduct;

(4) corporate governance oversight with respect to the implementation and effectiveness of the compliance and ethics programme;

(5) high level involvement with a specific individual assigned overall responsibility;

(6) conducting effective training programmes and otherwise disseminating information appropriately;

(7) monitoring, auditing, and evaluation of any compliance program;

(8) having and publicizing a system, which may include mechanisms that allow for anonymity or confidentiality, whereby the organization's employees and agents

may report or seek guidance regarding potential or actual criminal conduct without fear of retaliation;

(9) disciplinary measures.[18]

It should be borne in mind that the guidance will relate as much to the section 1   5.31 offence as it does to section 6 in as much as it concerns procedures operated by the company at the relevant time to prevent bribery.

C. PENALTIES

A corporate found guilty of this offence, which can only be tried on indictment, is   5.32 liable to pay an unlimited fine. There is no statutory guidance as to the appropriate level of fine, and it remains to be seen whether the Sentencing Guidelines Council will issue any guidance.

In addition, the corporate faces the prospect of having the proceeds of its criminal   5.33 conduct confiscated under Part 2 of the Proceeds of Crime Act 2002.

It was feared at one stage that a corporate convicted of this offence would also face   5.34 mandatory debarment under the EU Procurement Directive.[19] However, this is still to be determined.

This part of the Act is a wake-up call to corporates to scrutinize their procedures,   5.35 reassess their risks, take competent and timely advice, and implement a zero-tolerance policy when it comes to paying bribes—offered or demanded, large or merely small 'grease' payments.

Doubtless, responsible enterprises will be just as anxious to prevent their own   5.36 employees or agents from being bribed by, for example, their competitors. However, the Law Commission did not think it necessary to extend the requirement for adequate procedures to the receipt of bribes, concluding thus:[20]

It might seem odd to leave a gap in the coverage of corporate liability for a failure to prevent bribery where, for example, there has been a failure to prevent an employee *taking* a bribe. However, new criminal offences should extend no further than is necessary. The principal justification for the introduction of this offence is to deter companies from giving direct or indirect support to a practice or culture of bribe-taking on the part of those with whom they do business. Its main purpose is not to encourage companies to do more to prevent their employees and agents from acting in a corruptly self-interested way.

---

[18] See Sentencing Guidelines para 8B2.1 available at <http://www.ussc.gov/2009guid/> (last accessed 6 July 2010).
[19] Public Procurement Directive 2004/18/EC [2004] OJ L134/114.
[20] Law Commission (n 1 above) para 6.5.

6

DEFENCES

A. ADEQUATE PROCEDURES

Section 7 of the Act creates a wholly new offence applicable to a 'relevant commer-   6.01
cial organisation' ('the organization'). The offence is committed when a person
associated with an organization bribes another intending either to obtain or retain
business for the organization or to obtain or retain a business advantage for that
organization.

This is a strict liability offence, with a defence available to the organization if it   6.02
can prove that it had in place adequate procedures designed to prevent the briber in
question from undertaking such conduct.

This defence of 'adequate procedures' is dealt with fully in Chapter 5.   6.03

B. DEFENCE FOR ARMED SERVICES AND INTELLIGENCE SERVICES

In its efforts to reform the criminal law of bribery, the Government considered that   6.04
a defence was necessary for certain state actors who would otherwise be at risk of
prosecution under the Act when performing important functions on behalf of the
public. The defence under section 13 of the Act seeks to provide legal certainty for
members of the intelligence services and armed forces and is based in large part on
the Secretary of State's existing power to authorize the Secret Intelligence Service to
commit criminal offences and civil wrongs under the Intelligence Services Act 1994.
However, the OECD's Legal Director, Nicola Bonucci, noted that these provisions
may represent the only law in the world sanctioning bribery. In response, the then
Attorney General, Baroness Scotland of Asthal, contended, in what she made plain
were her provisional views on this defence, that the United Kingdom's intelligence
services, unlike those of many other countries, are regulated by statute, accountable
to Parliament, and subject to external scrutiny by independent Commissioners.

The Government has sought to temper criticism by noting that the defence has precedent in primary legislation—namely the defence available for particular child pornography offences in the Protection of Children Act 1978. The defence in section 13 is drafted in very similar terms to that in the 1978 Act.

6.05   Section 13 of the Act provides a defence for a person charged with a 'relevant bribery offence' to prove that his conduct was 'necessary' either for:

(a) the proper exercise of any function of an intelligence service; or

(b) the proper exercise of any function of the armed forces when engaged on active service.

6.06   Section 13(5) provides that a person's conduct is to be treated as 'necessary' in circumstances where the person's conduct would otherwise be an offence under section 2 and involves conduct on the part of another person which would amount to an offence under section 1 but for the defence in section 13(1). As the Explanatory Notes make plain, section 13(5) has the effect that a recipient of a bribe paid by a member of the intelligence services or armed forces is covered by the defence in any case where the person offering or paying the bribe is able to rely on the section 13 defence. The insertion of this subsection, on the day of enactment, was in response to a concern raised in committee by Lord Thomas of Gresford, whereupon he suggested that it would be invidious for two individuals to find themselves in the dock, one charged with an offence under section 1 and the other with an offence under section 2. The first person is a member of the intelligence services who had paid a bribe, while the second person accepted the bribe in return for providing some information or other assistance to his co-accused. It has always been the Government's policy intention that both individuals should be able to avail themselves of the defence. However, Lord Thomas had questioned whether the recipient of the bribe could meet the necessity test in section 13(1). On reflection, the Government agreed that the policy intention could be better expressed. Accordingly, section 13(5) makes it clear that if it is necessary in pursuit of a function of one of the intelligence services or armed forces for a bribe to be paid then it will be treated as necessary for the other person to receive it, thereby triggering the defence for the recipient of the bribe.

6.07   The Act *does not* provide for a system of prior ministerial authorization, removing the measure of ministerial oversight present in early drafts of the legislation. It is the Government's belief that the enacted defences provisions provide for a more 'focussed and case specific' mechanism than the authorization scheme.[1] The Government has confirmed that in place of prior authorization by ministers, the defence ensures that the necessity or otherwise of the conduct is tested by reference to the roles of individual people and the particular circumstances of individual cases.

---

[1] Letter to the Chairman of the Constitution Committee, in response to the Committee's report on clause 12, from Lord Bach, 27 January 2010.

1. 'Relevant Bribery Offence'

A 'relevant bribery offence' is any one of the following: 6.08

- An offence under section 1 which would not also be an offence under section 6. This removes the power to bribe foreign public officials and so removes any risk of non-compliance with the OECD Convention, since that Convention is limited to bribery of this kind. It does not, however, reduce the risk identified by the Joint Committee on the Draft Bribery Bill of non-compliance under the United Kingdom's broader convention obligations to the United Nations, the Council of Europe, and the European Union.[2] It is noteworthy that in confirming her view that international conventions were not offended by the inclusion of this defence, the former Attorney General cited those very 'important safeguards'—time-limited authorizations given personally by the Secretary of State—that were later removed by the Government.

- An offence under section 2.

- An offence committed by aiding, abetting, counselling, or procuring either of the above.

- An offence of attempting or conspiring to commit, or of inciting the commission of, either of the above.

- An offence under Part 2 of the Serious Crime Act 2007 (encouraging or assisting crime) in relation to either of the above.

2. Any Function of an Intelligence Service

'Intelligence service' means the Security Service, the Secret Intelligence Service, or   6.09
GCHQ. 'GCHQ' has the meaning given by section 3(3) of the Intelligence Services Act 1994. In that Act the expression 'GCHQ' refers to the Government Communications Headquarters and to any unit or part of a unit of the armed forces of the Crown which is for the time being required by the Secretary of State to assist the Government Communications Headquarters in carrying out its functions.

The head[3] of each intelligence service *must* ensure that the service has in place   6.10
arrangements designed to ensure that any conduct of a member of the service which would otherwise be a relevant bribery offence is necessary for the proper exercise of any function. Those arrangements must be considered to be 'satisfactory' by the Secretary of State, which will be an ongoing requirement.[4] It will be the responsibility of the head of each of the intelligence services and the Defence Council (see below) to design arrangements which will work most effectively for their staff and

---

[2] Joint Committee on the Draft Bribery Bill, *First Report of Session 2008–2009* (28 July 2009) para 199.

[3] 'Head' means (a) in relation to the Security Service, the Director General of the Security Service, (b) in relation to the Secret Intelligence Service, the Chief of the Secret Intelligence Service, and (c) in relation to GCHQ, the Director of GCHQ.

[4] *Hansard*, HL, col 1710 (8 April 2010).

operational activities. The Government indicated, by way of illustration, that such arrangements might include internal guidance on the offences and the defence, and on the taking of internal legal advice in specified circumstances.[5]

6.11   Concerns were raised during the passage of the Bill that the defence pertaining to the intelligence services was too broadly crafted. The House of Lords Select Committee on the Constitution twice reported its concerns regarding this offence. It highlighted the numerous statutory functions of the intelligence services with regard to national security, safeguarding the economic well-being of the United Kingdom, and assisting in the prevention and detection of serious crime. The Committee could not envisage a scenario in which the defence should apply where the intelligence services were acting to safeguard the economic well-being of the country. The Government's response was that it would be 'inappropriate to differentiate between these core functions . . . as to do so would undermine the ability of the Services to combat all relevant threats to the United Kingdom'. There is considerable overlap between these functions and it will not always be apparent, at least initially, to what function the conduct in question related. The Government gave examples of situations in which the intelligence services are required to take action to monitor events and trends that might have a serious effect on the UK economy as a whole. These could include intelligence on instability in a part of the world where substantial UK economic interests are at stake; threats to the supply of energy or other commodities vital to the UK economy; or external attempts to manipulate commercial markets, especially where such actions could undermine confidence in the City of London or the stability of other financial markets.

3. Any Function of the Armed Forces

6.12   'Armed forces' means Her Majesty's forces (within the meaning of the Armed Forces Act 2006). 'Active service' means service in (a) an action or operation against an enemy, (b) an operation outside the British Islands for the protection of life or property, or (c) the military occupation of a foreign country or territory.

6.13   The Defence Council *must* ensure that the armed forces have in place arrangements designed to ensure that any conduct of (a) a member of the armed forces who is engaged on active service, or (b) a civilian subject to service discipline when working in support of any person falling within paragraph (a), which would otherwise be a relevant bribery offence is necessary for the proper exercise of any function. As with the obligations on the intelligence service, these arrangements must be considered to be 'satisfactory' by the Secretary of State.

---

[5] House of Lords Select Committee on the Constitution Fourteenth Report, *Bribery Bill and Constitutional Reform and Governance Bill: Government Responses to the Committee's Seventh and Eleventh Reports of Session 2009–10* (29 March 2010). See also *Hansard*, HL, col 1708 (8 April 2010).

4. Burden and Standard of Proof

The Explanatory Notes to the Act state that although not explicit on the face of the   6.14
Act, in accordance with established case law, the standard of proof the defendant
would need to discharge in order to prove the defence is the balance of probabilities.
In its response to concerns raised by the Constitution Committee (for which see
above), the Government similarly confirmed that 'it is for the defendant to prove the
defence on the balance of probabilities in any case that reaches court'.

Lord Thomas of Gresford, shortly before enactment, contended that the burden   6.15
of proving this defence was 'impossible'. His contention followed his earlier submissions during the Act's passage, where he raised difficult questions in relation to the
burden of proving this defence:

To [prove that his conduct is necessary], if he is a member of the Security Service, he must inevitably have to go into his instructions, which are no doubt difficult to produce. He cannot walk
into MI5 offices and demand to see the documents to prove his defence-his instructions, the
structure, and so on. An impossible burden is placed on him. It may be slightly easier for a person
in the Armed Forces to have access to papers, but my experience of military courts martial is that
the prosecution is not overanxious to provide defendants with the necessary material. The burden
on him is impossible.[6]

He later went on to query: 6.16

How can a person charged at the Old Bailey conceivably put together a defence to show that his
conduct in bribing someone in Afghanistan was necessary for the proper exercise of a function of
the Armed Forces? Who can he call? Where are the documents? Where are the witnesses? It is just
impossible for that to be sustained. This defence is impossible to run on a practical level without
compromising the functions of the security services. It cannot work.[7]

Lord Elystan-Morgan also expressed concern, reminding the House that raising   6.17
this defence may mean having to go into the most sensitive areas of intelligence and
security: 'It may present a totally genuine and innocent person with an almost
impossible task. Why should that be so?'[8]

The Government has failed adequately to address these concerns, saying only that   6.18
when there is a suspicion that someone has committed the offence of bribery under
the Act, the prosecutor will first consider whether a charge should be brought, secondly look at the defence in section 13, and finally decide whether a prosecution
should be brought in those circumstances. If the prosecution decides, 'as they nearly
always will, one might surmise',[9] that a prosecution will not be brought because it
comes under the defence in section 13, the matter will not go to court. If, however,
the prosecutor decides that the case should go to court, because they are not satisfied
that it falls within section 13, the person prosecuted will have the further protection

---

[6] *Hansard*, HL, col 166 (2 February 2010).
[7] Ibid col 181.
[8] Ibid col 168.
[9] Ibid col 182.

of the jury. That person will have the chance to persuade a jury, on balance, that he is covered by section 13.

6.19 On the question of the 'impossibility' of proving that section 13 applies, Lord Bach said this on behalf of the Government:

> [T]he noble Lord, Lord Thomas, said that the defence cannot work. He assumes that the only value of the defence is in the course of the trial, but that is not the case. As well as providing the legal certainty we should be seeking for the intelligence services and Armed Forces, the defence provides a clear pointer for prosecutors when deciding whether or not to charge a person with an offence under the Bill. Can the defence work? The noble Lord thinks that it cannot, but Parliament has already approved something very similar in Section 1B (1)(b) of the Protection of Children Act 1978.[10]

6.20 Practitioners may empathize with Lord Thomas's response that 'we are not dealing with pornography' and agree that the analogy is an unhelpful one. The authors have been unable to locate any authorities dealing with the provision in the 1978 Act.

---

[10] Ibid.

7

FACILITATION PAYMENTS, CORPORATE HOSPITALITY, PROMOTIONAL EXPENDITURE, AND COMMISSION PAYMENTS

A. FACILITATION PAYMENTS

The law of England and Wales has never recognized 'facilitation payments' as a dis-   7.01
tinct category, ie a form of bribery worthy of being excepted from the general law
criminalizing such behaviour; the Bribery Act 2010 does not alter that position. The
default position therefore remains that facilitation payments, no matter how big or
small and no matter what they are called, still amount to bribery.

This is in contrast to the position in the United States where low value facilitation   7.02
payments to 'expedite or to secure the performance of a routine governmental
action'[1] are permitted only if the payments are not used to encourage a foreign
public official to award new business or to continue existing business. The statute
lists the following examples of 'routine governmental action': obtaining permits,
licences, or other official documents; processing governmental papers, such as visas
and work orders; providing police protection, mail pick-up and delivery; providing
phone service, power and water supply, loading and unloading cargo, or protecting
perishable products; and scheduling inspections associated with contract performance or transit of goods across country.

Paragraph 9 of the OECD Convention similarly provides that small 'facilitation'   7.03
payments do not constitute payments made 'to obtain or retain business or other

---

[1] 15 USC§§ 78dd-1(b), 78dd-2(b), 78dd-3(b).

improper advantage' within the meaning of paragraph 1 and, accordingly, are also not an offence. However, in its recommendations for further combating bribery of foreign public officials, adopted on 26 November 2009, the OECD Bribery Working Group recommended that, in view of the corrosive effect of small facilitation payments, particularly on sustainable economic development and the rule of law, member countries should:

(1) undertake to periodically review their policies and approach on small facilitation payments in order effectively to combat the phenomenon;

(2) encourage companies to prohibit or discourage the use of small facilitation payments in internal company controls, ethics, and compliance programmes or measures, recognizing that such payments are generally illegal in the countries where they are made, and must in all cases be accurately accounted for in such companies' books and financial records.

7.04   Practitioners should also note the emphasis placed upon 'facilitation payments' in the OECD's Phase 3 questionnaire.[2]

1. Definition

7.05   The Law Commission has assisted with this broad definition: 'it is generally accepted that a facilitation (or "speed" or "grease") payment is a payment made with the purpose of expediting or facilitating the provision of services or routine government action which an official is normally obliged to perform'.[3]

7.06   It should be noted that TRACE[4] has observed that the precise definition of facilitation payments is 'often unclear and stretched to breaking point'. The Law Commission[5] has set out various definitions; in framing their codes of conduct, companies may wish to consider the numerous definitions contained therein.

2. Guidance

7.07   In recognition of the need to reinvigorate efforts to combat facilitation payments, the OECD has recently issued a recommendation calling on member countries periodically to review their policies and approach to these small payments (see above). There are undoubtedly difficult and unanswered dilemmas facing business, as Lord Robertson illustrated before the Joint Committee on the Draft Bribery Bill: 'stevedores

---

[2] Available at <http://www.oecd.org/dataoecd/44/31/44685243.pdf> (last visited 15 June 2010). It should also be noted that the Working Group on Bribery has established a schedule of Phase 3 evaluations from 2009 to 2014, which includes the designation of two countries to act as lead examiners in each evaluation.

[3] Law Commission Consultation Paper No 185 (31 October 2007) Appendix F, para F.5.

[4] TRACE International Inc (TRACE) is a non-profit membership association that pools resources to provide practical and cost-effective anti-bribery compliance solutions for multinational companies and their commercial intermediaries.

[5] Law Commission (n 4 above), Appendix F.

on the docks of a country say they will not unload your ship unless a payment is made to their union or to their corporate organisation, what do you do? You say, "No. We will just let our ships lie there"[?]'.

The Government is expected to publish guidance imminently to assist businesses. 7.08 The following principles emerged from exhaustive parliamentary debate on this issue:

- If companies pay facilitation payments in order to gain a business advantage they run the risk of prosecution. Bribery on any scale cannot and should not be tolerated or condoned.[6]

- It may not be in the public interest to prosecute where payments are small; much will depend on the particular circumstances.[7]

- Prosecutorial discretion will be used to manage such payments in 'the real world'.

- The Government recognizes that many UK companies still struggle with petty corruption in emerging markets and other countries, facing regular demands for 'facilitation payments' in circumstances that amount to extortion or something very near. The Government's belief is that the answer is to face the challenge head-on, not to create exemptions and defences like those of the United States Foreign Corrupt Practices Act, which created artificial distinctions that are difficult to enforce and have the potential to be abused.[8]

- Prosecutors will take into consideration countervailing factors. These might include the small nature of the bribe, the options facing the payer, whether it was a single or repeated incident, whether the bribe was solicited in circumstances that were tantamount to extortion, and whether the court is likely to impose a nominal penalty.[9]

- Another relevant factor might be the cost to the public purse of prosecution, as well as where facilitation payments were paid in response to a physical threat to the health and safety of a company's employees. While a threat of commercial damage does not provide a defence in cases of bribery, the prosecuting authorities are likely to take into account any element of extortion when considering where the public interest lies.[10]

- A gratuity is not a bribe; it is usually paid as thanks for the proper performance of functions.[11]

---

[6] *Hansard*, HL, col 1087 (9 December 2009).
[7] Ibid col 1122.
[8] *Hansard*, HL, col 135 (2 February 2010).
[9] Ibid col 136.
[10] Ibid col 137.
[11] Ibid col 136.

7.09   In his response to the Joint Committee, the Director of the Serious Fraud Office (SFO) endorsed 'prosecutorial discretion, backed by appropriate guidance' as a means of dealing with facilitation payments:

Facilitation payments will be unlawful . . . [but] small facilitation payments are unlikely to concern the SFO unless they are part of a larger pattern (when, by definition, they would no longer be small facilitation payments) where their nature and scale has to be evaluated . . . The SFO considers, like Lord Woolf and a number of UK corporates, that any facilitation is unjustifiable and should be removed because these payments cut across transparency and openness. They also render a corporate (and other corporates) more vulnerable to demands for larger bribes. They are a major contributor to the belief that bribery is a necessary part of business culture.[12]

B. CORPORATE HOSPITALITY

7.10   The Law Commission has identified two of the business community's primary concerns in relation to corporate hospitality:[13]

(1) ensuring that conventional corporate hospitality practices should not fall into the ambit of bribery; and

(2) providing guidance on what kind and degree of corporate hospitality is or is not acceptable.

7.11   The Commission recognized that where, for example, a supplier provides corporate entertainment to regular customers, the purpose is normally to cement existing links with the customers, provide information, and keep the existence of the supplier at the forefront of the customers' minds when it comes to the placing of orders. In that sense it is clearly designed to assist in the acquisition and retention of business, and would be a pointless exercise if it were not. Where those entertained are employees of potential customers, and have responsibility for choosing among possible suppliers, the potential for bribery is present.[14]

7.12   It is generally accepted that corporate hospitality is a legitimate part of doing business at home and abroad, provided it remains within appropriate limits. To the extent that any corporate hospitality might be caught by these offences—which the Government certainly does not expect generally to be the case—it is appropriate for prosecutors to take a view on where the public interest lies.[15] It is unlikely that reasonable hospitality to foreign officials will attract the interest or action of enforcement authorities.[16] As with facilitation payments, the 'thorny issue' of corporate hospitality will be addressed in government guidance, initially expected in July 2010, but now predicted, with a change in government, to be delayed until 2011.

---

[12] Memorandum submitted by the Serious Fraud Office (BB 14).
[13] Law Commission, *Reforming Bribery* (Law Com No 313, 2008).
[14] Ibid D.14.
[15] *Hansard*, HL, col GC43 (7 January 2010).
[16] Ibid.

In a letter from Lord Tunnicliffe to Lord Henley dated 14 January 2010,[17] the 7.13
Government's position was clarified: the general bribery offences are based on an
improper performance test—corporate hospitality would therefore trigger the
offence only where it was proved that the person offering the hospitality intended
the recipient to be influenced to act improperly. Clearly, lavish or extraordinary
hospitality may lead a jury to reach such a conclusion but, as the Director of the
SFO told the Joint Committee, 'most routine and inexpensive hospitality would be
unlikely to lead to a reasonable expectation of improper conduct'.

Lord Tunnicliffe went on to confirm that: 7.14

> [the section 6] offence is formulated differently. It requires that the person offering the advantage
> must intend to influence the foreign public official in the performance of their functions and that
> the applicable written law neither permits nor requires the foreign public official to be influenced
> by the offer, promise or gift. (The bribe must also be intended to obtain or retain business or
> a business advantage). If there is no applicable written law which allows for hospitality in these
> circumstances, the offence may be committed.

The Government concluded that it is sufficient to rely on prosecutors to differen- 7.15
tiate between legitimate and illegitimate corporate hospitality and to decide whether
or not it would be in the public interest to bring a prosecution.

C. PROMOTIONAL EXPENDITURE

Promotional expenditure is an important part of modern business practice and the 7.16
Government has made plain that it is not seeking to restrict appropriate expenditure
of this kind.[18] Whether promotional expenditure will amount to an offence will
depend on the facts, although it is anticipated that some expenditure will be caught
by the provisions of this Act.

Promotional expenditure that is designed to explain and inform potential buyers 7.17
of a commercial organization's products may not involve the transfer of any advantages for the purpose of section 6.[19] However, if, for example, benefits that might be
regarded as hospitality are included within promotional expenditure, and the local
law does not expressly permit or require the receipt of such benefits by officials, the
expenditure may be caught by the section 6 offence. Whether such a case would
proceed would be subject to prosecutorial discretion.[20]

The Government has made plain that it is not its intention to drag a series of 7.18
companies through the courts on the basis of promotional expenditure that does not
seek simply to bribe a public official.[21] Nevertheless, the Confederation of British

---

[17] Available at <http://www.justice.gov.uk/publications/bribery-bill.htm>.
[18] *Hansard*, HL, col 127 (2 February 2010).
[19] Ibid.
[20] Ibid.
[21] *Hansard*, HC, col 47 (16 March 2010) per Claire Ward.

Industry (CBI) has raised two concerns: in its view, without any requirement for dishonesty in the Act, businesses either have to commit to no promotional expenditure, which is clearly unsustainable, or openly condone criminal acts by their staff on the basis that they will probably not be prosecuted, which is also unsustainable. Secondly, any proper promotional expenditure would, the CBI contends, irrespective of prosecutorial discretion under the Bribery Act, be a breach of section 328 of the Proceeds of Crime Act 2002 unless companies obtain consent from the Serious Organised Crime Agency (SOCA) to make each payment. This, the CBI states, is plainly unworkable. It is submitted that prosecution for money laundering is highly unlikely where the supposed predicate offence, committed by the use of promotional expenditure, is not itself the subject of prosecution. Where that conduct is not prosecuted by virtue of the sensible application of prosecutorial discretion, it is difficult to see in what circumstances the exercise of that same discretion would nevertheless permit a prosecution for money laundering.

D. COMMISSION PAYMENTS

7.19   In its final report the Law Commission[22] recalled that many brokers and agents are remunerated by a commission, payable by the supplier of the product sold, even though the agent is supposed to be acting for the buyer. The situation, the Commission conceded, has a superficial resemblance to bribery, in that the agent is performing duties for the buyer, but is motivated by the prospect of the commission (ie the advantage).

7.20   Much of the discussion in the Law Commission's Consultation Paper No 185 concerned the question of whether the commission was the primary reason for the agent's actions. In one sense, the Law Commission contended, it clearly is: if there were no commission the agent would not act at all. On the other hand, it said, the commission is not, or ought not to be, the agent's reason for recommending one product rather than another. If the agent deliberately recommended the most expensive product in order to maximize the commission, without regard to the interests of the client, that might arguably be corrupt.

---

[22] Law Commission (n 14 above).

8

CONSENT TO PROSECUTE

A. SECTION 10

Section 10 of the Act provides that a prosecution in England and Wales can only be   8.01
brought with the consent of the director of one of the three senior prosecuting
authorities:

(a) the Director of Public Prosecutions (DPP);

(b) the Director of the Serious Fraud Office; and

(c) the Director of Revenue and Customs Prosecutions.

    A prosecution in Northern Ireland can only be brought with the consent of the   8.02
DPP for Northern Ireland or the Director of the Serious Fraud Office.[1]

    The Director of the Serious Fraud Office may delegate his functions under this   8.03
section to an authorized member of staff. Other delegation powers already exist for
the other directors. There were concerns that without proper restrictions in place,
the decision to prosecute would be made by those too far down the prosecutorial
ladder. However, a late amendment to the Act[2] provided that the function of consenting to a prosecution <u>must</u> be exercised personally by the director of the relevant
prosecuting authority, and a director would not be able to delegate the function to
other prosecutors. An exception to that overarching provision enables the DPP, the
Director of the Serious Fraud Office and the Director of Revenue and Customs
Prosecutions to nominate another person to act when the director is unavailable.
The Explanatory Notes to the Act reflect what was determined during parliamentary debates, namely that 'unavailability' would be extremely restrictive in its scope,

---

[1] Section 10(2).

[2] Section 10(4).

limited, for example, to those situations in which the director is out of the country or is incapacitated.

8.04   In the case of the DPP for Northern Ireland, the amendment preserved the position whereby the deputy director has all the powers of the DPP, but neither the director nor deputy director will be able to delegate the consent function under the Act to another person.

B. REMOVAL OF CONSENT

8.05   Under the law as set out in the Public Bodies Corrupt Practices Act 1889 and the Prevention of Corruption Act 1906, prosecutions for bribery could not be commenced without the consent of the Attorney General. So-called consent cases are statutorily created with the requirement for consent to prevent certain offences from being prosecuted in inappropriate circumstances. In a memorandum to the 1972 Franks Committee, the Home Office set out five reasons why certain offences require consent:

To secure consistency in prosecution, e.g. where it is not possible to define the offence very precisely so that the law goes wider than the mischief aimed at or is open to a variety of interpretations; To prevent abuse or bringing the law into disrepute, because the offence is a kind which may result in vexatious private prosecutions; To enable account to be taken of mitigating factors, which may vary so widely from case to case that they are not susceptible to statutory definition; To provide some central control over the use of the criminal law when it has to intrude into areas which are particularly sensitive or controversial, such as race relations; and To ensure that prosecution decisions take account of important considerations of public policy or international nature such as may arise, for example, in official secrets or hijacking.

8.06   Section 10 removes the requirement to obtain the consent of the Attorney General before commencing criminal proceedings for a statutory bribery offence. This change reflects requests made by the OECD Bribery Working Group and by GRECO, the Council of Europe's monitoring body. It is a significant amendment to a practice that had been accepted for more than a century; one, indeed, that provoked strongly expressed feelings during the passage of the Bill through Parliament. Of particular concern were the questions of accountability to Parliament, prosecutorial discretion, delegation of authority, and, underpinning the whole debate, whether the removal of this single function should have been deferred until the fundamental review of the Attorney General's constitutional position had been completed. This was frustrated by the announcement of an election and the speedy ending of the parliamentary session.

C. ATTORNEY GENERAL'S POWER OF DIRECTION

8.07   The change does not affect the superintending role of the Attorney General over the main prosecuting authorities. Indeed, it was remarked by Lady Whitaker in

Grand Committee that 'the Attorney General has not been airbrushed out of the picture'.[3]

The protocol between the Attorney General and the prosecuting departments, **8.08** published in July 2009, sets out how the Attorney General and the prosecutors will work together to ensure that the Attorney General can discharge that responsibility.[4]

In her evidence to the Joint Committee on the Draft Bribery Bill, the former **8.09** Attorney General, Baroness Scotland of Asthal, noted that accountability will remain for as long as the Law Officers remain the supervisors and superintendents of the prosecutorial authority (Q626). She also noted that it is proposed that there should be a new protocol entered into between the directors and the Attorney General to clarify their relationship and duties towards each other—work on that was under-way at the time of publication. The protocol's self-professed purpose is to formalize the Attorney General's relationship with the prosecutorial directors.

D. THREE PROSECUTING AUTHORITIES

Section 10 envisages at least three routes by which a prosecution can be launched. **8.10** The danger, therefore, is of different thresholds of prosecution. Three people fulfill-ing a role that has previously been occupied by only one—the Attorney General—comes with the potential for conflicting prosecution policies. Even with set criteria for prosecution, interpretations can vary greatly. Concerns expressed throughout the Act's passage centred on the level of consistency to be expected in prosecution deci-sions and whether a difference of policy could creep in.

It is hoped that the protocol referred to above will assist in the harmonization of **8.11** prosecution policies when it comes to the exercise of prosecutorial discretion for Bribery Act offences.

---

[3] *Hansard*, HL, col GC 69 (7 January 2010).
[4] The protocol is available at <http://www.attorneygeneral.gov.uk> (last visited 15 June 2010).

9

OUTCOMES, PENALTIES, AND REMEDIES

A. OUTCOMES

The Act has bestowed no new powers upon any agency charged with investigating 9.01
or prosecuting bribery and corruption. However, to fulfil its role as lead agency in
the area of overseas corruption, the Serious Fraud Office (SFO) has set up a separate
work area, which it has called the Anti-Corruption Domain. Ultimately, the SFO
intends to have 100 staff working in this area.

In the last 18 months we have witnessed the discovery of bribery of overseas offi- 9.02
cials addressed in different ways by different agencies. In the case of Aon, a regulated
insurance broker, a fine was imposed by the Financial Services Authority (FSA) for
inadequate procedures and poor financial recording. In the case of Balfour Beatty,
the company was made the subject of a civil recovery order, again for a 'books and
records' offence. An individual prosecuted by the CoLP Overseas Anti-Corruption
Unit received an immediate prison sentence. Innospec, a US company with an
English subsidiary, was fined in both jurisdictions by prior agreement, and Robert
Dougall, the former employee of DePuy International who acted as an important
whistleblower willing to give evidence for the Crown, was given a prison sentence of
12 months, subsequently suspended on appeal.

These cases will all be dealt with in greater detail below but they are set out here to 9.03
demonstrate various techniques that are being employed in an attempt to counter corruption by large corporations in an efficient and cost-effective manner. Unfortunately,
it would appear that a number of tensions have emerged between different agencies

and between the United Kingdom and foreign countries, and in the United Kingdom itself, between the functioning of the executive and the judiciary. The FSA and the SFO, both under threat from the change of government, appear to be vying with one another for the titles of regulatory and enforcement champion. The SFO has invited self-reporting without having previously put in place a programme which could lawfully provide, if not immunity, then at least leniency for cooperating businesses; neither does it have the power to take the decision to prosecute and then defer taking that step so long as the errant corporation remains compliant but, in the event that it does not, compel it to plead guilty in the future.

9.04   The Act does not concern itself with anything other than the creation and punishment of offences. The impact statement which accompanied the Bill in Parliament made it clear that although prosecution should be easier, that did not mean that there would be more prosecutions (an increase of 1.3 cases per annum was envisaged) but that the Act would achieve its purpose by deterrence and, where that failed, prosecutorial discretion and judicial discretion would pursue an appropriate course to sanction the 'bad actors'.

1. Plea Bargaining

For all the respectable and reputable fronts that many fraudsters and corrupt businessmen may present, they are criminals. What is sometimes described as white collar crime or commercial crime taking the form of fraud and corruption in particular is crime. And it is not victimless: sometimes identified individuals are victims, and at others, unnamed, unknown individuals in the entire community are victims, and sometimes the community itself is the victim. So often however the criminal activities are buried under mountains of paper and myriads of figures so that the process of investigation, and ultimately any trial, requires huge resources and painstaking and sometimes protracted study, examination and analysis.[1]

9.05   The 'Guidelines on Plea Discussions' issued by the Attorney General in March 2009 were intended to address and, so far as possible, alleviate those very problems identified by the Lord Chief Justice in the *Dougall* case. However, those guidelines do not alter the position that in the UK jurisdiction, a plea agreement or bargain between the prosecution and the defence in which they agree what the sentence should be, or present what is in effect an agreed package for the court's acquiescence, is contrary to principle. That applies to cases of this kind, as it does to others. The guidelines are framed in unequivocal language:

(a) Where a plea agreement is reached, it remains entirely a matter for the court to decide how to deal with the case. [A9]

(b) Where agreement is reached as to pleas, the parties should discuss the appropriate sentence with a view to presenting a joint written submission to the court. This document should list the aggravating and mitigating features arising from the agreed facts, set out any personal mitigation available to the defendant, and refer to any relevant sentencing guidelines

---

[1] *R v Dougall* [2010] EWCA Crim 1048, the Lord Chief Justice.

or authorities. In the light of all of these factors, it should make submissions as to the applicable sentencing range in the relevant guidelines [D9] . . . in the course of the plea discussion the prosecutor must make it clear to the defence that the joint submission as to sentence (including confiscation) is not binding on the court. [D12]

(c) . . . The prosecution should send the court sufficient material to allow the judge . . . to assess whether the plea agreement is fair and in the interests of justice, and to decide the appropriate sentence. It will then be for the court to decide how to deal with the plea agreement. In particular, the court retains an absolute discretion as to whether or not its sentences in accordance with the joint submission from the parties [E4 and E5]

See 9.24 below for a fuller consideration of the issues arising where a cooperating accomplice enters into an agreement under the Serious and Organised Crime and Police Act 2005. 9.06

2. Self-reporting

The SFO has recently sought to provide additional guidance with respect to its policies on self-reporting.[2] The proclaimed benefit to the corporate will be the prospect (in appropriate cases) of a civil rather than a criminal outcome as well as the opportunity to manage the issues and any publicity proactively. A negotiated settlement rather than a criminal prosecution also means that the mandatory debarment provisions under Article 45 of the EU Public Sector Procurement Directive[3] in 2004 will not apply. 9.07

Following a 'self-report' the SFO will want to establish the following: 9.08

(1) Is the Board of the corporate genuinely committed to resolving the issue and moving to a better corporate culture?

(2) Is the corporate prepared to work with the SFO on the scope and handling of any additional investigation considered to be necessary?

(3) At the end of the investigation (and assuming acknowledgement of a problem) will the corporate be prepared to discuss resolution of the issue on the basis, for example, of restitution through civil recovery, a programme of training and culture change, appropriate action where necessary against individuals, and at least in some cases external monitoring in a proportionate manner?

(4) Does the corporate understand that any resolution must satisfy the public interest and must be transparent? This will almost invariably involve a public statement although the terms of this will be discussed and agreed by the corporate and the SFO.

(5) Will the corporate want the SFO, where possible, to work with regulators and criminal enforcement authorities, both in the United Kingdom and abroad, in order to reach a global settlement?

---

[2] Available at <http://www.sfo.gov.uk/bribery--corruption/self-reporting-corruption.aspx> (last visited 6 July 2010).

[3] Directive 2004/18/EC [2004] OJ L134/114.

9.09   So far as individuals are concerned, examples of the questions the SFO would ask are:

(1) How involved were the individuals in the corruption (whether actively or through failure of oversight)?

(2) What action has the company taken?

(3) Did the individuals benefit financially and, if so, do they still enjoy the benefit?

(4) If they are professionals should the SFO be working with the appropriate disciplinary bodies?

(5) Should the SFO be looking for directors' disqualification orders?

(6) Should the SFO think about a serious crime prevention order?

9.10   In discussing settlement terms, once satisfied with the conclusion of the investigation, the SFO will consider the following:

(1) restitution by way of civil recovery to include the amount of the unlawful property, interest, and costs;

(2) in some cases monitoring by an independent, well-qualified individual nominated by the corporate and accepted by the SFO. The scope of the monitoring will be agreed with the SFO, which will undertake that if monitoring is needed, it will be proportionate to the issues involved;

(3) a programme of culture change and training agreed with the SFO;

(4) discussion, where necessary, and to the extent appropriate, about individuals.

9.11   In addition, a public statement agreed by the corporate and the SFO will be needed so as to provide transparency as far as possible for the public.

9.12   The SFO notes that there will be many occasions when the corruption issue discovered gives rise to potential liability in other jurisdictions as well. The SFO appreciates that corporates in these circumstances want finality at international as well as domestic level and therefore will discuss with the corporate whether it wants assistance and involvement in a settlement with other authorities.

9.13   In the face of the Act, corporates may choose to approach the SFO for further guidance on adequate procedures. In any discussions about procedures within the corporate the SFO will be looking to find evidence of adequate procedures to assess how successful the corporate has been in mitigating risk. The SFO will also be looking closely at the culture within the corporate to see how well the processes really reflect what is happening in the corporate. For example, the SFO will look for the following:

(1) a clear statement of an anti-corruption culture fully and visibly supported at the highest levels in the corporate;

(2) a Code of Ethics;

(3) principles that are applicable regardless of local laws or culture;

(4) individual accountability;

(5) a policy on gifts and hospitality and facilitation payments;

(6) a policy on outside advisers/third parties including vetting and due diligence and appropriate risk assessments;

(7) a policy concerning political contributions and lobbying activities;

(8) training to ensure dissemination of the anti-corruption culture to all staff at all levels within the corporate;

(9) regular checks and auditing in a proportionate manner;

(10) a helpline within the corporate which enables employees to report concerns;

(11) a commitment to making it explicit that the anti-bribery code applies to business partners;

(12) appropriate and consistent disciplinary processes;

(13) whether there have been previous cases of corruption within the corporate and, if so, the effect of any remedial action.

B. PENALTIES

1. Individuals

Any offence under the Act committed by an individual under section 1, 2, or 6 is punishable as follows: 9.14

- On indictment: an unlimited fine or imprisonment for up to 10 years or both.
- Upon summary conviction in England and Wales: a fine and/or up to 12 months' imprisonment.
- Upon summary conviction in Northern Ireland: a fine and/or up to six months' imprisonment.

It should be borne in mind that these provisions will also apply to senior officers who fall foul of the 'consent or connive' provisions,[4] whereby the offence committed is not a separate one of 'consenting or conniving' but is in fact the 'main' bribery offence. 9.15

Section 154 of the Criminal Justice Act 2003, which is not yet in force, sets the maximum sentence that can be imposed by a magistrates' court in England and Wales at 12 months. Where an offence under this Act is committed before section 154 comes into force, the magistrates' court's power is limited to six months.[5] 9.16

The maximum penalty for an individual has been increased from seven years to 10 years to reflect the seriousness of the offences contained within the Act. 9.17

---

[4] Section 14.
[5] Section 154(4)(a) of the Criminal Justice Act 2003.

In increasing the maximum period of imprisonment, the Government adopted the recommendation of the Law Commission, which noted that there was a significant 'perverse incentive' to charge fraud instead of bribery in the most serious cases, because the maximum penalty (10 years' imprisonment) was higher than it was for bribery (seven years' imprisonment).

9.18   Further, the United Kingdom is a party to the OECD Convention, Article 3.1 of which requires the signatories to apply criminal penalties which are 'effective, proportionate and dissuasive'.

2. Non-individuals

9.19   An offence committed by a person other than an individual is punishable by a fine. In either case, the fine may be up to the statutory maximum (£5,000) if the conviction is summary, and unlimited if it is on indictment. The section 7 offence can only be tried upon indictment.

9.20   The Government has undertaken to consider whether it would be appropriate to ask the Sentencing Council to issue guidance on sentencing for bribery offences.

C. SENTENCING AUTHORITIES: THE OLD LAW

1. Domestic Bribery

9.21   The following table contains summaries of only a selection of the sentencing authorities applicable to offences under the old law, which are likely to continue to inform sentencing decisions under the new legislation.

Case	Detail	Sentence
R v Ozakpinar [2008] EWCA Crim 875, [2009] 1 Cr App R (S) 8	The offender, who was chief procurement officer for the CPS, was convicted of corruption in respect of employing persons who were personal friends and receiving payments in connection with three separate contracts.	30 months' imprisonment. The Court of Appeal did not accept an argument that guidelines for theft in breach of trust were helpful in dealing with corruption cases.
R v Welcher [2007] EWCA Crim 480, [2007] 2 Cr App R (S) 519	Two men were convicted of conspiracy to corrupt and conspiracy to defraud. They had been involved in paying sums of money of the order of £3 million to an employee of a major company, in return for showing favour to the offenders' company by placing major orders and authorizing overpayments to the company.	6.5 years' imprisonment.

Case	Detail	Sentence
R v Bush [2003] EWCA Crim 1056, [2003] 2 Cr App R (S) 117 (p 686)	The defendant, who worked for a London borough, was convicted of corruption contrary to common law. He approached a person who ran a company which repaired and installed heating systems and water equipment and offered to put the company on the council's contracts list so that it could tender for larger jobs for the council. The defendant asked for payments of £100 per week. The other man agreed and made payments over a period of about six years. The defendant was not in a position to guarantee that the company would be successful in tendering, but he was able to nominate the company so that it would be given the opportunity to tender. In addition to the regular weekly payments, the appellant asked for specific payments on occasion, and other services were provided. Eventually the payments ceased; the company was removed from the approved contractors' list and went into liquidation. The total benefits derived by the defendant amounted to about £40,000.	On appeal, the court noted that the defendant's corrupt conduct persisted over a period of six years: 'It represented on any view a gross abuse of trust of his position as a public servant and was motivated by greed'. Nevertheless, on all the authorities a sentence of four years' imprisonment was manifestly excessive. Sentence reduced to 2.5 years.
R v Anderson [2002] EWCA Crim 2914	A man employed as a manager by a company agreed to accept a payment of £25,000 from a company supplying services to his employer, in return for arranging that contracts were placed with the company concerned. Monies were paid on a small but regular basis into a company which the defendant and an accomplice had set up, and false invoices were created, which did not relate to any work actually carried out. A total of £23,650 was paid into the new company's account, of which £8,500 was paid to the defendant.	12 months' imprisonment, reduced to six months on appeal.
R v Dearnley and Threapleton [2001] 2 Cr App R (S) 42	The defendants were convicted of corruption. The first defendant was employed by a metropolitan council with responsibility for property management. The second defendant's companies provided security services to the council over a period of several years and received payments of approximately £1 million for services	In allowing an appeal against sentence, the Court of Appeal cautioned that it is seldom a surprise when corrupt individuals prove to be of hitherto good character: 'Were it otherwise they would, in general, not be in a position from which to behave in a fashion which strikes at the

(Continued)

Case	Detail	Sentence
	rendered over a period of years. The second defendant supplied to the first a car valued at £5,445. The first defendant secured a loan from the council to pay for the car, and used the money so obtained to clear debts.	principle of fair competition. Public confidence in people such as these appellants is undermined, irrespective of the amounts pocketed by an individual, by virtue of the evil which is corruption. Custody is inevitable; it is rightly seen as a deterrent to those tempted to depart from their usual scrupulous standards'. Sentences of 18 months' imprisonment reduced to 12 months for both defendants, described as 'broken men'.
R v Donald [1997] 2 Cr App R (S) 272	A detective-constable in a regional crime squad pleaded guilty, at a late stage of his trial, to four counts of corruption. He had accepted various sums of money from a man against whom criminal proceedings were being brought to disclose confidential information about the inquiry and to destroy surveillance logs. The officer had agreed to accept approximately £50,000 and actually received about £18,500.	11 years' imprisonment. The sentencing judge commented that the case was 'almost unique' in its seriousness. The Court of Appeal said the sentence was severe, but not manifestly excessive: 'The learned judge felt that a sentence was required which would mark in unmistakable terms the peril which would attend anyone failing to perform his duty in this way and she was, in our judgment, right to do so'.
R v Bennett and Wilson [1996] 2 Cr App R (S) 879	The defendants were convicted respectively of receiving and giving a bribe on two occasions. The first defendant was employed in a government department with responsibility for the procurement of publicity material. The second appellant was the managing director of a group of companies involved in supplying printing work to the department. Over a period of about two years the second defendant made available to the first defendant two company cars, at the expense of the second defendant's company.	The Court of Appeal noted that corruption, as found by the jury, between individuals in the position of Bennett and Wilson should always be regarded as a serious crime: 'As the judge rightly observed, it strikes at the principle of fair competition, and it undermines public confidence in the rectitude of public servants and those who are in a position to grant or to assist in the granting of significant contracts involving public money. Moreover, for any who may be tempted to be less than absolutely scrupulous, the expectation of a custodial sentence should act as a deterrent'. Nine months' imprisonment reduced, on the particular facts of the case, to four months.

Case	Detail	Sentence
R v Foxley [1995] 2 Cr App R 523	The defendant was employed by the Ministry of Defence, with direct influence over the placement of all substantial contracts for ammunition. He was convicted of 12 counts of corruption contrary to section 1 of the Prevention of Corruption Act 1916 for corruptly placing contracts with three foreign manufacturing companies.	Concurrent terms of four years' imprisonment on each count.
R v Patel (1992) 13 Cr App R (S) 550	An administrative officer for the Home Office (a man of good character) working in its Immigration and Nationality Department admitted that he had accepted a payment of £500 to stamp a passport with leave to remain in the country.	Two years' imprisonment.
R v Hopwood (1985) 7 Cr App R (S) 402	The defendant pleaded guilty to one count of corruption and was convicted of four counts. He was a director of a company which required supplies of steel. He accepted the rewiring of his house in return for ordering steel from a supplier whose steel was of inferior quality, and later accepted sums of money totalling more than £200,000 and other gifts in return for failing to disclose a fraud being carried out against his employers by a third party: the fraud cost his employers about £1.75 million over a period of several years.	The Court of Appeal noted that 'Corruption on this scale does great injury to the commerce of this country. Those who are in positions of trust like this appellant must be brought to book for their corrupt practices and punished severely. One of the oddities of this branch of the law is that the maximum sentence under the Act for conduct of this kind is two years' imprisonment for any particular act of corruption. [It has since been increased to seven years.] The facts of this case might indicate that perhaps the time has come for the maximum sentence to be reviewed by Parliament. If this kind of corruption spreads it will be a cancer in our commercial and industrial life. It is the duty of this Court, in our judgment, to make it clear that those who are in positions of trust, like this appellant was should expect little in the way of mercy from the courts'. In dismissing the defendant's appeal, Lawton LJ commented that the defendant was, 'exceedingly lucky to have ended up with no more than a total of three and a half years' imprisonment'.

(Continued)

Case	Detail	Sentence
R v Wilson (1982) 4 Cr App R (S) 337	The appellant, a 38-year-old man of previous good character, was convicted of conspiracy to commit corruption and three counts of corruption. The appellant was a purchasing agent and chief buyer with a large manufacturing concern who received considerations worth about £2,500, either in the form of money or a holiday, in return for showing favour to a company supplying parts to his employer.	Sentence of 3.5 years' imprisonment reduced to 18 months on appeal.

2. Foreign Bribery: Individuals

9.22   At the time of publication there have been only two successful prosecutions for foreign bribery, one brought on behalf of the City of London Anti-Corruption Unit, and one on behalf of the SFO. The latter was the subject of an appeal against sentence[6] and is considered at para 9.24 below.

9.23   In August 2008, Neils Tobiasen, the 65-year-old Danish managing and financial director of CBRN Team, a UK-based weapons security company, pleaded guilty to one count of bribery under the 1906 Act. The director had paid £83,000 in bribes in 2007–2008 to two Ugandan officials in relation to a £210,000 contract. In September 2008, Tobiasen received a five-month jail sentence suspended for one year. Judge James Wadsworth QC, sitting at Southwark Crown Court, suspended Tobiasen's sentence after hearing how he had given a 'full and frank' confession soon after his arrest and had cooperated with the prosecution. The judge said he accepted that Tobiasen had paid the bribes in response to the Ugandan officials' demands and that the scheme was 'very far' from his own idea. The scheme was instead instigated by Ananias Tumukunde, a private secretary in the Ugandan Government's science and technology department, who was jailed for one year, following a guilty plea to a charge of accepting corrupt payments. Judge Wadsworth recommended that Tumukunde be deported at the end of his jail term.

9.24   In April 2010, British businessman Robert Dougall, a former vice president of DePuy International, a health equipment manufacturer owned by Johnson & Johnson, pleaded guilty to a single charge of conspiracy to corrupt Greek health officials. He was the first British businessman to be prosecuted by the SFO for paying bribes to foreign officials. Mr Justice Bean, sitting at Southwark Crown Court, sentenced Dougall to 12 months' imprisonment, despite requests from both the defence and prosecution that imprisonment be suspended. The court heard that Dougall had pleaded guilty at the earliest stage of the investigation into DePuy and had agreed to testify against former colleagues in possible future prosecutions in the

---

[6] *R v Dougal* [2010] EWCA Crim 1048.

United Kingdom and United States. However, Mr Justice Bean said that although Dougall had been 'of great value to the SFO, criminality on that scale' could not merit anything other than immediate imprisonment. The judge gave Dougall leave to appeal the decision because of the public interest issues raised by the case; he certified that the case was fit for appeal on the basis that it raised 'a novel point on the proper approach to sentence in cases involving an agreement with the cooperating defendant under section 73 of [the Serious Organised Crime and Police Act] 2005'.

The Court of Appeal heard the appeal on 29 April 2010 and judgment was passed on 13 May. The court emphasized the seriousness of the offence, recording what Kofi Annan, the Secretary General to the United Nations, observed in his foreword to the 2003 UN Convention Against Corruption:

9.25

Corruption is an insidious plague that has a wide range of corrosive effects on society. It undermines democracy and the rule of law, leads to violations of human rights, distorts markets, erodes the quality of life and allows organised crime, terrorism and other threats to human security to flourish. This evil phenomenon is found in all countries—big and small, rich and poor . . . corruption hurts the poor disproportionately by diverting funds intended for development, undermining a government's ability to provide basic services, feeding inequality and injustice and discouraging foreign aid and investment. Corruption is a key element in economic underperformance and a major obstacle to poverty alleviation and development.

The court recognized that this was a case which involved substantial international corruption. The court was careful not to allow the issue of guidelines for the prosecution of cases of fraud and corruption to suggest that they were more respectable than other forms of crime, or to be persuaded that somehow those who committed fraud or corruption should not be ordered to serve prison sentences because such sentences should be reserved for those they would regard as common criminals: 'once convicted, those are the ranks that they join'. The court went on to confirm that in this jurisdiction a plea agreement or bargain between the prosecution and the defence in which they agreed what the sentence should be, or presented what was in effect an agreed package for the court's acquiescence, was contrary to principle, and that that applied to cases of this kind, as it did to others. At the core of the judgment was the warning that responsibility for the sentencing decision in cases of fraud or corruption is vested *exclusively* in the sentencing court (or on appeal, from that court, to the Court of Appeal Criminal Division). There are no circumstances in which it may be displaced. In the present case, while suspending the period of imprisonment imposed by Mr Justice Bean, the court opined that a suspended sentence should only be imposed where there are particular features of a defendant's involvement in the crime, including the matters of mitigation, which justify it. That, it said, is fact specific.

9.26

In providing guidance for sentencing judges, the court indicated that where the appropriate sentence for a defendant whose level of criminality, and features of mitigation, combined with a guilty plea, and full cooperation with the authorities investigating a major crime involving fraud or corruption, with all the consequent

9.27

burdens of complying with his part of the SOCPA agreement, would be 12 months'
imprisonment or less, the argument that the sentence should be suspended is very
powerful. This result will normally follow. Their Lordships concluded that given all
the circumstances this was an appropriate case for the sentence of 12 months' imprisonment on the defendant to be suspended.

3. Foreign Bribery: Companies

9.28   At the time of publication, there has been no appellate consideration of the sentence
to be imposed upon a company for the bribery of foreign public officials. However,
on 18 March 2010, Innospec Ltd, a UK company and a wholly owned subsidiary of
a Delaware company, pleaded guilty to conspiracy to corrupt, contrary to section 1
of the Criminal Law Act 1977. Sentence was subsequently passed by Thomas LJ,
sitting at the Southwark Crown Court. Innospec had conspired with its directors
and others to make corrupt payments, contrary to section 1 of the Prevention of
Corruption Act 1906, to public officials of the Government of Indonesia to secure
contracts from that Government for the supply of Tetraethyl lead (TEL). Discussions
began with US prosecuting authorities with a view to achieving what was to be
described as a 'global settlement'. The SFO soon became a party to those discussions. Both the SFO and Department of Justice (DOJ) agreed that they should not
seek to impose a penalty that would drive the company out of business. Discussions
culminated in an offer by Innospec Inc to pay $25.8 million, with a further
$14.4 million contingent upon the performance of certain contracts. The sum was
put forward in full and final settlement of all outstanding issues with the DOJ, the
Securities and Exchange Commission (SEC), the Office of Foreign Assets Control
(OFAC), and the SFO. The offer was accepted subject to the approval of the courts
in the United States and United Kingdom. This was the first case where a 'global
settlement' had been sought in respect of concurrent criminal proceedings in the
United Kingdom and United States. It was appreciated that the case was highly
unusual, because only a small fraction of the penalties that could properly be imposed
would be sought in light of Innospec's ability to pay. It is essential to refer to the
judgment of Thomas LJ for a précis of the ways in which the agreements were presented to each court. What is of particular import is Thomas LJ's conclusion that the
SFO cannot enter into an agreement under the laws of England and Wales with an
offender as to the penalty in respect of the offence charged. One reading of the joint
sentencing submission and plea agreement would, he concluded, suggest that a penalty had in fact been agreed. He ended the judgment thus: 'I have concluded that the
Director of the SFO has no power to enter into the arrangements made and no such
arrangements should be made again'.

9.29   On 25 September 2009, Mabey & Johnson Ltd appeared at Southwark Crown
Court for sentence in relation to admitted offences of overseas corruption and
breaching UN sanctions. The company is to pay a total of £6.6 million. This was the
first prosecution brought in the United Kingdom against a company for these
offences. The company, which is a supplier of steel bridging and is based in Twyford,

Berkshire, had already indicated at a magistrates' court hearing on 10 July 2009 that it would plead guilty to these offences. The prosecution for corruption arose from the company's voluntary disclosure to the SFO of evidence to indicate that the company had sought to influence decision-makers in public contracts in Jamaica and Ghana between 1993 and 2001. The decision voluntarily to disclose the corruption offences to the SFO was taken by the management of Mabey & Johnson's holding company in February 2008, whereupon an investigation was opened. The prosecution for breach of UN sanctions during 2001/02, as they applied to contracts in the Iraq 'Oil-for-food' programme, arose from an investigation commenced in January 2007. During the course of these investigations the company cooperated with the SFO.[7]

D. CONFISCATION AND CIVIL RECOVERY

A bribery conviction under the Act triggers the court's power to impose a confiscation or civil recovery order (CRO) under the Proceeds of Crime Act 2002 (POCA). These powers can be used to recover all the proceeds of a crime, which can have a particularly punitive effect in relation to bribery offences; the confiscation order imposed upon Mabey & Johnson, for example, totalled £1.1 million—that is in addition to a fine of £3.5 million, reparations of £1.4 million, costs of £350,000, and an undertaking to undergo monitoring at its own expense for several years. The Joint Committee on the Draft Bribery Bill provided the much starker example of an individual who makes a buyout offer worth £15 million to a company's shareholders, and who pays a bribe of £50,000 to a chief executive to secure his endorsement of the buyout. That individual risks losing the entire value of the company and its assets if he acquires it due to the bribe succeeding. That is, the penalty for paying a bribe of £50,000 could be as high as £15 million.[8]   9.30

So far as confiscation is concerned, the 2003 Joint Committee on the draft Corruption Bill queried whether confiscation in such cases is wrong in principle and whether it would in fact be a violation of the First Protocol to the European Convention on Human Rights (ECHR). The Ministry of Justice has since stated that the courts could be relied upon not to operate confiscation powers in a way that contravenes human rights legislation. During the passage of the Bill, it was suggested that companies convicted of offences under the Bribery Act should not be vulnerable to POCA confiscation orders for fear that the amounts thereof would be destructive of the whole business enterprise. The Government saw no reason to treat corrupt businesses any differently from any other offender subject to a confiscation order. Lord Tunnicliffe responded to Lord Henley's queries on the matter by   9.31

---

[7] For the relevant 'opening notes', see <http://www.sfo.gov.uk/media/41953/sfo-annex2-statement-01-250909.pdf> and <http://www.sfo.gov.uk/media/41964/sfo-annex2-statement-02-250909.pdf> (both last visited 15 June 2010).

[8] Para 186.

stating: 'Under the Proceeds of Crime Act 2002, the exercise of confiscation powers is directed towards the recovery of the proceeds of crime. It is not intended to be punitive in effect. We are satisfied that the courts will take into account all relevant information'.[9] Stakeholders have since reiterated the importance of the combined powers to fine and to confiscate being exercised in a way that remains 'proportionate and reasonable'. That civil powers should operate in such a manner was subsequently required of the Government by the Joint Committee.

9.32   The POCA permits an 'enforcement authority' to apply to the High Court for a CRO under Part 5 of that Act. An enforcement authority may be the Director of the Serious Organised Crime Agency, the Director of Public Prosecutions, the Director of Revenue and Customs Prosecutions, or the Director of the Serious Fraud Office. If the enforcement authority proves to the civil standard the existence of 'property obtained through unlawful conduct' ('recoverable property') or property that represents recoverable property, the court may make an order vesting the property in a trustee for civil recovery. If it is in the interests of justice the SFO will use its civil recovery powers as a suitable alternative to instituting criminal proceedings. The Attorney General issued guidance for use of these powers on 5 November 2009. The guidance cautions that care must be taken not to allow an individual or body corporate to avoid a criminal investigation and prosecution by consenting to the making of a CRO, in circumstances where a criminal disposal would be justified under the overriding principle that the reduction of crime is generally best served by that route, and in accordance with the public interest factors in the relevant prosecutors' code. Nevertheless, the guidance does concede that civil recovery represents a better deployment of resources to target someone with significant property which cannot be explained by legitimate income.

1. Balfour Beatty Plc

9.33   On 6 October 2008, Balfour Beatty Plc agreed to pay £2.25 million under a CRO agreed with the SFO. This was the first time the SFO used the asset-seizing powers it gained in April 2008. Having itself brought matters to the attention of the SFO, Balfour Beatty accepted that unlawful conduct, in the form of inaccurate accounting records arising from certain payment irregularities, occurred within a subsidiary entity, during the construction of The Bibliotheca Project in Alexandria, Egypt, completed over seven years previously. The project was undertaken by a Balfour Beatty subsidiary in a joint venture with an Egyptian company. The unlawful conduct related to entries in a subsidiary company's records in respect of payment irregularities, in respect of the execution of the contract. The documentation prepared in connection with these payments did not comply with the requirements for accurate business records to be kept in accordance with section 221 of the Companies Act 1985. Once Balfour Beatty had discovered and investigated these payments,

---

[9] *Hansard*, HL, Vol 716, col GC52 (7 January 2010).

it immediately notified the SFO. In a consent order agreed before the High Court, Balfour Beatty agreed to a settlement payment of £2.25 million together with a contribution towards the costs of the CRO proceedings. Balfour Beatty also voluntarily agreed to introduce certain compliance systems, and to submit these systems to a form of external monitoring for an agreed period.

2. AMEC

On 26 October 2009, the SFO obtained a CRO of almost £5 million against AMEC Plc, an international engineering and project management firm. AMEC made a referral to the SFO in March 2008 following an internal investigation into the receipt of irregular payments. The payments, which were made between November 2005 and March 2007, were associated with a project in which AMEC was a shareholder. The SFO determined that unlawful conduct occurred in connection with the description entered into AMEC's books and records of the payments in question, which amounted to failure to comply with the requirements of section 221 of the Companies Act 1985. The SFO acknowledged that upon completion of the internal investigation AMEC acted promptly and responsibly in referring the case and cooperated with the SFO's investigation into the corporate irregularities. In a consent order agreed before the High Court, AMEC agreed to a settlement payment of £4,943,648 plus the costs incurred as a result of the civil recovery proceedings.

9.34

The following text discusses financial reporting orders and serious crime prevention orders, which were both designed to discourage and disrupt recidivist career criminals. However, there is no legal reason why these orders should not be made, all other considerations being equal, in the case of those accused, and/or convicted, of serious corruption offences.

9.35

E. FINANCIAL REPORTING ORDERS

By virtue of the Serious Organised Crime and Police Act 2005, section 76(1) and (2), a court sentencing an offender for an offence listed in section 76(3), which has been amended to include the new bribery offences under sections 1, 2, and 6 of the 2010 Act, may also make a financial reporting order in respect of that offender, provided it is satisfied that the risk of the person committing another offence of the kind mentioned in section 76(3) is sufficiently high to justify the making of the order.

9.36

The purpose of a financial reporting order is to require the person on whom the order is imposed to make a report to a specified person as to such particulars of his financial affairs as may be specified in the order.[10] The report may relate to a specified period of time beginning with the date on which the order comes into force and

9.37

---

[10] Section 79(3).

to subsequent specified periods of time, each beginning immediately after the end of the previous one.[11] Each report must be made within a number of days after the end of the period in question, as specified in the order.[12]

9.38　　A financial reporting order comes into force when it is made and has effect for the period specified in the order, beginning with the date on which it is made. If made by a magistrates' court, the period must not exceed five years.[13] If made by the Crown Court, the period must not exceed 20 years where the person has been sentenced to imprisonment for life, or 15 years in any other case.[14]

9.39　　A person who without reasonable excuse includes false or misleading information in a report, or who otherwise fails to comply with any requirement of section 79, is guilty of an offence and liable on summary conviction to imprisonment for a term not exceeding 51 weeks, or to a fine not exceeding level 5 on the standard scale, or to both.[15]

9.40　　Section 80 provides for the variation and revocation of financial reporting orders by the court which made the order, and section 81 provides for verification and disclosure of such orders.

9.41　　In *R v Adams*[16] the Court of Appeal determined that a financial reporting order is a sentence as it is an order made on conviction. A financial reporting order is not, however, a penalty for the purposes of Article 7 of the ECHR; it is a preventative measure intended to enable the courts to keep control over those in respect of whom there is the risk that they may indulge in criminal activity. Accordingly, there is no question of a bar on retrospective application of the provisions of section 76(1).

9.42　　In *R v Banki*[17] financial reporting orders were quashed after the Court of Appeal concluded that the judge 'could not have been satisfied that there was any risk, let alone a sufficiently high risk of the defendants committing a subsection (3) offence', after she concluded that she had to 'pass deterrent sentences, not to deter each of you gentleman, who I have no doubt will not come back before these courts again'.

9.43　　In *R v Wright*[18] the Court of Appeal noted that while this form of order is newly created it ought not to be thought that it is routinely to be made without proper thought:

We do not seek to set out any general rules for when it will be appropriate or not. This is not the right place in which to do that. No doubt the paradigm case for such an order is the defendant with a history of unsatisfactory business or financial dealing who at some stage at least is likely to be at large and engaged in business, commercial or financial activity which would otherwise be unsupervised or unmonitored. But it is perfectly clear that the section embraces also the appellant who is going to be a prisoner and, at least in the case of the very exceptional facts of this prisoner,

---

[11] Section 79(2).
[12] Section 79(5).
[13] Section 76(6).
[14] Section 76(7).
[15] Section 79(10).
[16] [2008] EWCA Crim 914, [2009] 1 WLR 301.
[17] [2008] EWCA Crim 2985.
[18] [2008] EWCA Crim 3207.

we have no doubt that an order can be appropriate. We are quite sure that judges who are asked to make financial reporting orders should give careful consideration to whether it would actually achieve anything. They should certainly look at alternative powers which are available to financial investigators if they would have much the same effect.

F. SERIOUS CRIME PREVENTION ORDERS

The Serious Crime Act 2007 ('SCA') provided for a new type of civil order, serious crime prevention orders (SCPOs), imposed by the High Court or Crown Court and designed to protect the public by preventing, restricting, or disrupting involvement in serious crime. SCPOs can include extensive restrictions and requirements and may run for a period of up to five years. Prohibitions, restrictions, and requirements can also be placed on bodies corporate, partnerships, and unincorporated associations.   9.44

1. Imposing an SCPO in the High Court

In order to impose an SCPO under section 1 of the SCA, the High Court (a) must be satisfied that a person has been involved in serious crime (whether in England and Wales or elsewhere) and (b) must have reasonable grounds to believe that the order would protect the public by preventing, restricting, or disrupting involvement by the person in serious crime in England and Wales.   9.45

A person is treated as 'involved in serious crime' if: 9.46

(1) he has a conviction for a serious offence. A list of serious offences is set out in Part 1 of Schedule 1 to the SCA. (The list is amended by the Bribery Act to ensure that the new bribery offences under sections 1, 2, and 6 constitute 'serious offences' for the purposes of the Serious Crime Act); or

(2) he has facilitated the commission by another person of a serious offence; or

(3) he has conducted himself in a way that was likely to facilitate the commission by himself or another person of a serious offence in England and Wales (whether or not such an offence was committed).

In applying the 'facilitation' provisions, the court must ignore acts that the respondent can show to be reasonable and, subject to that exception, it must also ignore his intention or any other aspect of his mental state at the time the offence was committed.[19]   9.47

Criminal conduct which takes place outside the jurisdiction may be taken into account.[20]   9.48

---

[19] Section 4(2) and (3).
[20] Sections 1(1)(a), 2(4) and (5).

2. Imposing an SCPO in the Crown Court

9.49 The Crown Court has a power to impose an SCPO where a person has been *convicted* of a serious offence in England and Wales either in the Crown Court or in a case where a magistrates' court has committed the matter for sentence, and if it has reasonable grounds to believe that the order would protect the public by preventing, restricting, or disrupting involvement by the person in serious crime in England and Wales. The Crown Court can make an order in addition to sentencing the person in relation to the offence or conditionally discharging him.[21] Proceedings in relation to SCPOs can be adjourned even after sentencing.[22] The court is not limited to evidence which would have been admissible in the criminal prosecution.

3. Prohibitions, Restrictions, or Requirements

9.50 An order under section 1 may contain such prohibitions, restrictions, or requirements and such other terms as the court considers 'appropriate' for the purpose of protecting the public by preventing, restricting, or disrupting involvement by the person concerned in serious crime in England and Wales.[23] Non-exhaustive examples of the type of provision that may be made by an SCPO are contained in section 5 of the SCA. An SCPO may include, *inter alia*, prohibitions or restrictions on an individual's financial dealings, working arrangements, access to premises (including his dwelling), and travel arrangements. It may also regulate the means by which an individual communicates or associates with others, and may require the individual to answer certain questions and produce certain documents.

4. Nature of the Proceedings

9.51 Proceedings in the High Court and the Crown Court are civil proceedings[24] and the standard of proof is the civil standard. Part 77 of the Civil Procedure Rules 1998 make provision for applications in the High Court for or relating to SCPOs. The Crown Court, when exercising its jurisdiction in relation to SCPOs, is a criminal court for the purposes of procedure rules and practice directions.[25] Part 50 of the Criminal Procedure Rules ('Civil Behaviour Orders after Verdict or Finding') applies to SCPOs by virtue of rule 50.1.

5. Safeguards and Limitations

9.52 Sections 6 to 10 contain general safeguards in relation to the making of such orders. There are restrictions on who may be the subject of an order,[26] who may apply for

---

[21] Section 19(7).
[22] Section 36(1)(b).
[23] Section 1(3).
[24] Sections 35 and 36.
[25] Section 36(4).
[26] Sections 6 and 7.

an order[27] and on the making of an order which may affect a third party without that party being given an opportunity to be heard.[28] Section 10 provides that a person is only bound by an order (or a variation of an order) if he is represented at the proceedings at which the order (or the variation) is made or if notice setting out the terms of the order has been served on him.

Sections 11 to 15 contain restrictions on the information that may be required under the terms of an order and limit the use to which information obtained under an order may be put. Provisions include restrictions in relation to: (i) answering questions or providing information orally; (ii) legal professional privilege; (iii) excluded material and banking information; and (iv) other enactments.   9.53

G. DEBARMENT

Needless to say the possibility of debarment will feature prominently in considerations on how to structure a settlement in multi-jurisdictional investigations. Of particular concern is the Public Procurement Directive ('the 'Directive').[29] Article 45 of the Directive provides: 9.54

Any candidate or tenderer who has been the subject of a conviction by final judgment of which the contracting authority is aware for one or more of the reasons listed below *shall* be excluded from participation in a public contract.

The following offences are listed: 9.55

(a) participation in a criminal organization, as defined in Article 2(1) of Council Joint Action 98/733/JHA;

(b) corruption, as defined in Article 3 of the Council Act of 26 May 1997[30] and Article 3(1) of Council Joint Action 98/742/JHA respectively;[31]

(c) fraud within the meaning of Article 1 of the Convention relating to the Protection of the Financial Interests of the European Communities;

---

[27] Section 8.

[28] Section 9.

[29] Directive (EC) 2004/18 on the coordination of procedures for the award of public works contracts, public supply contracts and public service contracts [2004] OJ L134/114.

[30] Article 3 states:

   (1) For the purposes of this Convention, the deliberate action of whosoever promises or gives, directly or through an intermediary, an advantage of any kind whatsoever to an official for himself or for a third party for him to act or refrain from acting in accordance with his duty or in the exercise of his functions in breach of his official duties shall constitute active corruption

   (2) Each Member State shall take the necessary measures to ensure that conduct of the type referred to in paragraph 1 is made a criminal offence.

[31] Which states '(1) For the purposes of this Joint Action, the deliberate action of whosoever promises, offers or gives, directly or through an intermediary, an undue advantage of any kind whatsoever to a person, for himself or for a third party, in the course of the business activities of that person in order that the person should perform or refrain from performing an act, in breach of his duties, shall constitute active corruption in the private sector'.

(d) money laundering, as defined in Article 1 of Directive (EC) 91/308 of 10 June 1991 on prevention of the use of the financial system for the purpose of money laundering.[32]

9.56 Unlike previous EU public procurement directives, where debarment was optional, Article 45 *mandates* the exclusion of suppliers convicted of these offences. Regulation 23 of the Public Contracts Regulations 2006[33] implements Article 45 in England. Paragraph 2 of regulation 23 accords very limited discretion to contracting authorities to disregard the prohibition only in cases where there are 'overriding requirements in the general interest which justify doing so'. In the United States, on the other hand, debarment is *clearly* discretionary.

9.57 In its report,[34] the Joint Committee on the Draft Bribery Bill noted that while debarment can be an effective deterrent/penalty in appropriate circumstances, the rigid policy imposed by regulation 23 creates problems. Neither the seriousness of the offence nor any mitigating factors can be taken into account. There is no mitigation for 'self-cleansing' under the regulation, which means that a company might face debarment for acts that took place many years in the past. The Committee concluded that the Government must 'take action at a European level to prevent companies being automatically and perpetually debarred following a conviction, while exploring shorter-term measures to prevent disproportionate penalties being imposed in the meantime. The Government must ensure that the UK reaches a position where debarment is discretionary, if self-reporting is to work effectively in practice'.[35]

The Secretary of State for Justice acknowledged the problems posed by debarment and assured the Joint Committee that he would look into ways of addressing the issue. During the Bill's passage, the Government was repeatedly challenged on this issue. On 3 March 2010, the House of Commons was assured that the Government was 'giving active consideration to whether conviction for the new corporate offence of failure to prevent bribery—the clause 7 offence—would require mandatory exclusion under the directive'.[36] Claire Ward, then Parliamentary Under Secretary of State, cautioned that this is 'not a straightforward issue, and there are a number of complex points that we need to consider. There is obviously a difference of view among European Union member states on how some aspects of the directive are being applied, but [the Government] will continue to look into the matter in further detail before coming to a view on it'. When pressed for some indication for business on where the Government stands on the issue of debarment, Claire Ward reaffirmed that the Government was aware that that is a serious issue and that companies are keen to know what will happen: 'we are working on this complex issue in relation to clause 7, and we hope to be able to reach a view on it shortly. However, I can

[32] [1991] OJ L166/77.
[33] SO 2006/5.
[34] 16 July 2009.
[35] Ibid para 192.
[36] *Hansard*, HC, col 982 (3 March 2010).

assure hon. Members that the Government's position will be clear before any of the offences are brought into force'.[37] Businesses may be able to take a measure of comfort from Lord Bach's recognition that under section 7, the culpable conduct on the part of the organization is not bribery in itself but rather a failure to prevent bribery.[38]

Practitioners should also be aware that a specialist Defence Procurement Directive agreed in January 2009 also makes reference to the treatment of suppliers convicted for corruption, with special clauses on security of supply. 9.58

Having regard to the understandable corporate anxiety about the vulnerability to mandatory debarment and the commitment by the corruption champion in the outgoing Government to use his best efforts to have Article 45 mitigated, it is probably unlikely that the new UK Government will regard conviction under section 7 of the Bribery Act as triggering debarment. It will, however, be necessary to canvas the views of the European Commission, and possibly of individual states within the European Union to ensure that this view is uniformly accepted. 9.59

The recent settlements with Siemens and BAE Systems demonstrate that care must be taken to sanction multi-national businesses with large public works departments in a way which punishes adequately but does not become a corporate death sentence. There is quite clearly a balancing act to be arrived at between the punishment of delinquent corporations and the need to preserve jobs, social cohesion, and retain economic value at a time of severe financial constraint. 9.60

One further consequence for corporates must be the impact on future funding support from multilateral development banks. An agreement for the Mutual Enforcement of Debarment Decisions between multilateral development banks was entered into on 9 April 2010. It provides for the cross-debarment of companies found to have committed fraud or corruption on contracts and projects financed by any one of these banks. The banks flexed their muscles for the first time on 30 April 2010 when Macmillan Publishing was declared ineligible to be awarded bank-financed contracts for a period of six years in the wake of the company's admission of bribery. 9.61

---

[37] Public Bill Committee, col 126 (18 March 2010).
[38] *Hansard*, HL, col 1124 (9 December 2009).

10
INVESTIGATION AND PROSECUTION

A. INVESTIGATION OF BRIBERY AND CORRUPTION

The United Kingdom has 43 separate police forces, a Serious and Organised Crime   10.01
Agency (SOCA), a Serious Fraud Office (SFO), a Financial Services Authority
(FSA), a Revenue and Customs Prosecution Office (RCPO), a Crown Prosecution
Service (CPS), and a Department for Business, Innovation and Skills (BIS). All of
these organizations may consider investigating bribery and corruption, although
only a few are specifically tasked with doing so.

Of the police forces, only the City of London force has a dedicated Overseas Anti-   10.02
Corruption Unit. It has already had at least one high profile success (for which see
Chapter 9), and it works closely with the CPS. The Unit is headed by a Detective
Chief Superintendent and staffed by specially trained officers with ring-fenced
resources.

B. THE SERIOUS FRAUD OFFICE

The lead agency tackling overseas corruption is the SFO, which not only investigates   10.03
and prosecutes bad actors in the United Kingdom, but is also kept busy rendering
assistance to agencies around the world. Its most recent reputational set-back was
the Government-inspired decision by its then Director in December 2006 to terminate an SFO investigation into BAE Systems. By way of background, on 29 July
2004 the Director of the SFO had launched an investigation into allegations of corruption against BAE Systems Plc ('BAE'). One aspect of the investigation concerned
what is known as the Al Yamamah contract, a valuable arms contract between Her
Majesty's Government and the Kingdom of Saudi Arabia for which BAE was the
main contractor. There followed a catalogue of 'interventions' by members of the

Government and other interested parties. These culminated in an announcement, on 14 December 2006, that, in light of the need to safeguard national and international security, the matter would be discontinued. It was emphasized repeatedly that no weight had been given to commercial interests or to the national economic interest; the Director was precluded from taking such considerations into account by Article 5 of the OECD. The House of Lords held that the Director's decision to discontinue the prosecution could not be impugned on the grounds that it was perverse, and so the decision stood.[1] However, as discussed in Chapter 12, there was disquiet that the United Kingdom may have acted in breach of its treaty obligations under the OECD Convention.[2] The SFO has recently come under close scrutiny in relation to another decision affecting BAE and its employees and agents, and very recently for the manner in which it dealt with so-called global settlements and plea bargaining. The SFO has been working closely with the Department of Justice (DOJ), an agency with many times the resources of the SFO and with powers far wider than those currently bestowed on its UK counterpart. The SFO has struggled to devise a strategy that accommodates the DOJ's power to encourage self-reporting and self-enquiry by companies, as well as the DOJ's ability to levy massive fines, impose the threat of deferred prosecution, and insist that corporations employ professional monitors at their own expense, but with a duty to report directly to the DOJ. The SFO has no such powers. It is trying to encourage self-reporting and will give credit, but not necessarily a non-criminal outcome, as a reward.[3] Where, as in the recent prosecution of Innospec—a US parent with a UK subsidiary—it has agreed to a level of fine compatible with that levied in the United States, it has been criticized for usurping the functions of the judiciary, and their exclusive right to determine the level and severity of any sentence. In that case, the trial judge deemed the financial penalty too lenient but nonetheless approved it having regard to the corporate expectations that had been created.[4]

10.04   Because cases of international corruption are expensive to investigate and prosecute, the SFO, in common with other agencies, relies upon encouraging whistleblowers who were themselves active participants in the offences. In the recent case of Robert Dougall, the former senior executive of DePuy International—a UK-based subsidiary of Johnson & Johnson—the court expressed itself unhappy that the SFO had purported to tie the court's hands on sentence in return for Dougall's cooperation.[5]

---

[1] *R (Corner House Research and others) v Director of the Serious Fraud Office* [2008] UKHL 60.
[2] Article 5 of the OECD Convention states: 'Investigation and prosecution of the bribery of a foreign public official . . . shall not be influenced by considerations of national economic interest, the potential effect upon relations with another State or the identity of the natural or legal persons involved'.
[3] The SFO's Guide on self-reporting can be found at <http://www.sfo.gov.uk/media/110693/approach%20of%20the%20serious%20fraud%20office%20v5.pdf> (last visited 6 July 2010).
[4] *R v Innospec Limited*, available at <http://www.judiciary.gov.uk/docs/judgments_guidance/sentencing-remarks-thomas-lj-innospec.pdf> (last visited 6 July 2010).
[5] *R v Dougall* [2010] EWCA Crim 1048.

A number of cases involving other jurisdictions are currently in the pipe-line.   10.05
While wishing to encourage self-reporting, the SFO has a limited menu of outcomes
with which to tempt corporations into self-reporting accompanied by full confes-
sions. Its performance in relation to the new offences might be enhanced were it to
be given wider and quasi-regulatory powers, similar to those of its US cousin.

Of course, self-reporting may not always be the result of some moral epiphany.   10.06
The UK's anti-money laundering laws, particularly those dealing with the regulated
sector, require the reporting of knowledge or suspicion of money laundering to the
Serious Organised Crime Agency (SOCA). Any suspicious activity report (SAR)
involving knowledge or suspicion of overseas corruption will find its way to the
SFO. The SFO has power to compel the handing-over of information in any form
and can compel the attendance of those it wishes to interview.[6] It can conduct
searches and seize evidence. It is hampered by not having a dedicated police force
but can and does call upon resources from the major local constabularies.

C. OTHER AGENCY INVOLVEMENT

While bribery is not a core concern of the FSA, it has been shown in the case of Aon   10.07
Ltd that the FSA will punish companies it regulates for failing to establish and maintain effective systems and controls to counter the risk of bribery associated with
making payments to overseas individuals and businesses.[7] This is in line with its
earlier policy of fining financial services companies for similar failings in connection
with anti-money laundering compliance. The FSA cannot presently prosecute
offences of bribery.

The SOCA is concerned with bribery only where there is a serious organized   10.08
crime element. However, it may also assist overseas agencies seeking evidence in the
United Kingdom and/or the extradition of suspects. It is, after all, the only truly
national police force.

Since governments in the developed world are keen to staunch the flow of taxable   10.09
income and gains to low tax or no tax jurisdictions, this is an area in which the RCPO
may become involved. International cooperation in this area is increasing apace.

---

[6] Criminal Justice Act 1987, s 2.

[7] In January 2009, the FSA fined Aon Ltd £5.25 million for failing to take reasonable care to establish and
maintain effective systems and controls to counter the risks of bribery and corruption associated with making
payments to overseas firms and individuals. Aon Ltd cooperated fully with the FSA and agreed to settle at an early
stage of the FSA's investigation. The firm qualified for a 30 per cent discount under the FSA's settlement discount
scheme. Without the discount the fine would have been £7.5 million. In announcing the fine, Margaret Cole,
director of FSA enforcement, said: 'This is the largest financial crime related fine imposed by the FSA to date. It
sends a clear message to the UK financial services industry that it is completely unacceptable for firms to conduct
business overseas without having in place appropriate anti-bribery and corruption systems and controls. The
involvement of UK financial institutions in corrupt or potentially corrupt practices overseas undermines the
integrity of the UK financial services sector. The FSA has an important role to play in the steps being taken by
the UK to combat overseas bribery and corruption. We have worked closely with other law enforcement agencies
in this case and will continue to take robust action focused on firms' systems and controls in this area'.

Those who used only to advise and service the super-rich and keep their tax bills low, are increasingly being targeted by politically exposed persons (PEPs), their families, and friends, who wish to use their services for the object of concealing their ill-gotten gains from the prying eyes of their governments. The exchange of information between tax authorities, as well as the purchase by tax authorities of stolen databases, make the discovery of laundering methods of corrupt politicians and officials ever more transparent. Furthermore, such developments have made it more likely that the identity of the briber as well as the bribee will be revealed.

D. EXTRADITION AND MUTUAL LEGAL ASSISTANCE

10.10   In addition to assisting overseas authorities with information, the United Kingdom has in the last seven years become a much easier place from which to secure the surrender of fugitive suspects. Jeffrey Tesler, a London solicitor, is at present appealing an order of a district judge that he be surrendered to the United States for allegedly laundering a large amount of money used to pay off Nigerian officials and politicians in connection with the development of the Bonny Island refinery project in Nigeria.

10.11   As bribery generates financial gain, it is an obvious predicate offence for sections 327 to 329 of the Proceeds of Crime Act 2002. These three money laundering sections each carry a maximum sentence of 14 years' imprisonment, with five years being the maximum sentence for those who merely fail to report knowledge or suspicion to a financial investigation unit.

10.12   The number of investigative agencies has increased and their powers have become more sophisticated. Mutual legal assistance spreads across the globe and may be procured far easier and faster than hitherto. Memoranda of understanding (MOUs) exist with a number of countries and authorities. They are intended to operate, together with letters of request, where no formal mutual legal assistance treaties or conventions are in place. Mutual recognition of foreign judicial acts and changes to the hearsay rules (the relevant provisions are sections 116 and 117 of the Criminal Justice Act 2003) also make it easier to present the information at trial. All that now stands in the way of a vigorous and robust, albeit fair, enforcement of the Bribery Act 2010 is the political will to hand the relevant agencies the means to finish the job.

11

MISCELLANEOUS PROVISIONS
IN THE ACT

A. APPLICATION TO THE CROWN

The Law Commission's draft Bribery Bill made no provision regarding application to the Crown. However, section 16 expressly applies the Act to individuals in the public service of the Crown. Such individuals (Crown servants) will therefore be liable to prosecution if their conduct in the discharge of their duties constitutes an offence under the Act.   11.01

B. CONSEQUENTIAL AMENDMENTS

Section 17, together with Schedules 1 and 2, make a number of repeals, revocations, and consequential amendments. Of particular import is the abolition of the common law offences of bribery and embracery, and the offences under the law of Scotland of bribery and accepting a bribe. The three Prevention of Corruption Acts are repealed in their entirety.   11.02

Section 17(4) to (10) creates a power for the Secretary of State (or, as the case may be, Scottish Ministers) to make supplementary, incidental, or consequential provision by order. The power includes power to make transitional, transitory, or saving provisions and to amend, repeal, revoke, or otherwise modify any provision made by or under an enactment, which includes Acts of the Scottish Parliament and Northern Ireland legislation. This order-making power is subject to the affirmative resolution   11.03

procedure[1] where it amends a public general Act or devolved legislation, otherwise the negative resolution procedure[2] applies. It has been submitted by the Ministry of Justice that this provides the appropriate level of parliamentary scrutiny for the powers conferred by section 17.[3]

11.04   The Ministry of Justice has conceded that the powers conferred by section 17 are wide; they create in effect a free-standing power to make consequential provisions at any time, including a power to amend primary and secondary legislation. The Ministry has recalled, however, that the powers are tied directly to the purposes of the Act or in consequence of it. There are numerous precedents for such provisions, including section 333 of the Criminal Justice Act 2003, section 173 of the Serious Organised Crime and Police Act 2005, section 51 of the Police and Justice Act 2006, and section 148 of the Criminal Justice and Immigration Act 2008. The Act, the Ministry has stated, makes significant changes to existing primary legislation (derived from a number of historical enactments) and it is possible that not all of their consequences have been identified in the Act's preparation.[4] Section 17 makes provision for such omissions.

C. EXTENT

11.05   Section 18 provides that the Act extends to England, Wales, Scotland, and Northern Ireland and that the amendments, revocations, or repeals contained within Schedules 1 and 2, except in relation to the Civil Aviation Act 1982, have the same extent as section 18. However, subsection (3) provides that the amendment of and repeals in the Armed Forces Act 2006 do not extend to the Channel Islands and subsection (4) provides that the amendments of the International Criminal Court Act 2001 apply only to England, Wales, and Northern Ireland.

D. COMMENCEMENT

11.06   The commencement and transitional provisions are contained in section 19 of the Act. The following sections came into force upon Royal Assent (8 April 2010):

(1)   section 16: application to the Crown;

(2)   section 17(4) to (10): the power to make supplementary, incidental, or consequential provision by order;

---

[1] Both Houses of Parliament must expressly approve the draft order before the order can be made. They have 40 days to consider it first. They can also (within 30 days) recommend upgrading the procedure to super-affirmative.

[2] The order may be made unless Parliament either disagrees within 40 days of laying or (within 30 days) recommends one of the other procedures.

[3] Memorandum by the Ministry of Justice to the Delegated Powers and Regulatory Reform Committee (November 2009).

[4] Ibid.

(3) section 18: extent;

(4) section 19(1) to (4): commencement;

(5) section 20: short title—the Act will be cited as the Bribery Act 2010.

The remainder of the Act will be brought into force by one or more commence- 11.07
ment orders made by the Secretary of State. Commencement orders are not subject
to any parliamentary procedure. As the Ministry of Justice has noted,[5] Parliament
has approved the principle of the provisions to be commenced by their enactment;
commencement by order enables the provisions to be brought into force at an
appropriate time. Any such order may appoint different days for different purposes,
and may make such transitional, transitory, or saving provision as the Secretary
of State considers appropriate in connection with the coming into force of any
provision of the Act.

The Government has indicated that it will publish guidance required by section 9 11.08
well in advance of section 7 coming into force, the intention having initially been
that it should be published before the Summer Recess 2010. That being the case, the
Government did not envisage bringing the offence under section 7 into force before
1 October 2010 at the earliest. The change in government has prompted a delay both
in enforcement and in the provision of guidance until Spring 2011 at the earliest.

Despite objection from the Law Society of Scotland, the Scottish Government 11.09
agreed in November 2009 that it was in the interests of good governance and an
effective justice system that the provisions of the Act, so far as these matters fall
within the legislative competence of the Scottish Parliament, should be considered
by the UK Parliament.[6] Section 19 nevertheless provides that the Secretary of State
must consult the Scottish Ministers before making an order under this section
in connection with any provision of this Act that would be within the legislative
competence of the Scottish Parliament if it were contained in an Act of that
Parliament.

E. TRANSITIONAL PROVISIONS

The Act does not affect any liability, investigation, legal proceeding, or penalty for 11.10
or in respect of a common law offence of bribery or embracery or the common law
offence in Scotland of accepting a bribe where it is committed wholly or partly
before the coming into force of the abolition provision (section 17). Nor does it
affect any liability, investigation, legal proceeding, or penalty for or in respect of an
offence under the Public Bodies Corrupt Practices Act 1889 or the Prevention of
Corruption Act 1906 committed wholly or partly before the coming into force of
the repeal of the Act by Schedule 2. This is in accordance with the general principle
that criminal offences should not have retrospective effect and ensures that offences

---

[5] Ibid.
[6] Legislative Consent Memorandum PB/S3/09/183 (November 2009).

which are committed wholly or partly before the commencement of the new provisions will fall to be prosecuted under the old law.

11.11   An offence is partly committed before a particular time if any act or omission which forms part of the offence takes place before that time. The Ministry of Justice, in its memorandum to the Joint Committee on the Draft Bribery Bill,[7] gave the example of an agreement made before the commencement date that a series of payments as part of a corrupt bargain will be paid in the future. This can be prosecuted as a substantive bribery offence or possibly a conspiracy to bribe, depending on the precise circumstances, under the old law. The future payments, the Ministry submitted, if taking place after commencement, may well, depending on the circumstances of the case, amount to a series of separate bribes and therefore be susceptible to the new provision. In the alternative, if the court took the view that the future payments were all part of a single scheme that began before commencement, then the conduct would fall to be dealt with under the old law.

F. SECONDARY AND INCHOATE LIABILITY

11.12   Where the context permits and the elements of the offence allow, ordinary principles of criminal law prevail and there may be secondary liability by way of such offences as aiding, abetting, counselling, or procuring. Similarly, liability may arise for inchoate offences such as encouraging and assisting the commission of offences, as well as for offences of attempting or conspiring to commit, or of inciting the commission of a bribery offence.

---

[7] Additional memorandum submitted by the Ministry of Justice (BB 53) (June 2009).

12

INTERNATIONAL AND DOMESTIC INSTRUMENTS

A. OVERVIEW

In enacting the Bribery Act 2010, Her Majesty's Government was putting beyond   12.01
doubt the UK's compliance with international instruments to which it has over time
adhered. The greatest emphasis was placed on the OECD Convention because, time
and time again, the United Kingdom has found itself the subject of public criticism
by that body, albeit couched in suitably diplomatic language. While it must not be
thought that the United Kingdom has a poor record in fulfilling its international
obligations, it must nevertheless be pointed out that at the time of the decision to
terminate the BAE Systems inquiry by the Serious Fraud Office (SFO), it was alleged
that the reasons for aborting the case were less to do with evidential insufficiency, or
even national security, and more motivated by the United Kingdom's strong economic ties with Saudi Arabia. That reason, if true, would put the United Kingdom
in clear breach of Article 5 of the OECD Convention.[1] The Convention has played,
and continues to play, a significant role in all the organizations whose instruments are
described below. Practitioners advising state parties will be rewarded by familiarity
with the instruments relevant to the issue in hand and most of the organizations

---

[1] Article 5 of the OECD Convention states: 'Investigation and prosecution of the bribery of a foreign
public official . . . shall not be influenced by considerations of national economic interest, the potential effect
upon relations with another State or the identity of the natural or legal persons involved'.

have staff ready to assist with explanations and advice. This is particularly important in the areas of mutual legal assistance and asset recovery. It is also noteworthy that many of the instruments are in a state of almost permanent development.

B. FOREIGN CORRUPT PRACTICES ACT 1977

12.02 The model for modern 'supply-side' efforts to combat the bribery of foreign public officials is the US Foreign and Corrupt Practices Act 1977 (FCPA). This was the legislators' response to what had been called the 'Tanaka-Lockheed scandal', involving the giant US defence contractor, which was uncovered almost by accident by investigators of the Watergate cover-up. A morally outraged Congress agreed to criminalize US public companies that were not transparent in their accounting records in relation to the payment of bribes to foreign public officials. What was contemplated was simply a 'books and records' offence, which would be met by an administrative fine. In order that US companies could start with a 'clean-sheet', they were asked to self-report in return for immunity from prosecution. The US lawmakers were both astonished and horrified when in excess of 400 US corporations owned up to having paid bribes to overseas officials at one time or another. The moral backlash fathered the offence sections of the FCPA, the decision that investigation should be with the FBI and prosecution with the Department of Justice (DOJ), with the Securities and Exchange Commission retaining its 'books and records' role. Congress was persuaded, with some hesitation, that small payments made to low-level officials for carrying out their normal duties would be exempted. These 'grease payments' have remained exempt and indeed persuaded those framing the OECD Convention 20 years later to make the same concession. However, three decades or more on, facilitation payments are now seen as repetitive bribes which support a systemic culture of corruption and encourage the payment of low wages to public officials while continuing to foster low commercial ethical standards. The OECD has now undertaken to persuade its members, including the United States, to reconsider the continuance of such payments and it is likely that more countries will join with the United Kingdom in supporting businesses in refusing to be blackmailed into making these payments. Clearly, this highlights one of the shortcomings of supply-side regulation.

12.03 The FCPA witnessed benign enforcement in the first two decades of its existence. However, since it was amended to incorporate the provisions of the OECD Convention, there has been considerably heightened activity, with the DOJ aggressively targeting not only US companies and their officers and employees, but also foreign companies caught within their jurisdictional remit. The DOJ has extracted massive fines ($1.5 billion from Siemens of Germany, $400 million from BAE Systems, and $600 million from Halliburton/KBR), imposed deferred prosecution agreements, employed monitors paid for by the target corporations, and prosecuted some companies and many individuals to conviction, usually securing in the case of the latter, lengthy prison sentences. As a role model for the SFO, the DOJ has the power to immunize or show leniency for self-reporting, encourage self-investigation by the delinquent company and await its outcome, and will be persuadable to impose sanctions that do not lead to either mandatory or discretionary exclusion.

The Act criminalizes the bribery of foreign public officials for business reasons   12.04
and further sanctions corporations whose bookkeeping is so deficient that bribes are deliberately or inadvertently concealed. The Act originally applied only to payments originating inside the United States, but was extended in 1998 to reach bribes originating outside the country as well. US companies are now liable for the acts of foreign employees. The Act contains both civil and criminal penalties (with a maximum penalty of 20 years' imprisonment). Some idea of prosecutorial activity can be gathered from the fact that in 2009, 38 individuals were charged by the DOJ and four by the SEC, with 15 corporate matters issued in the same year.

The anti-bribery provisions of the Act—sections 78dd-1, dd-2, and dd-3—make   12.05
it a crime for:

(1) an issuer of certain public securities or for any agent of such issuer

(2) to offer or give something of value to

(3) a foreign official and

(4) with the intent to corruptly influence an official act or decision, induce an action in violation of a lawful duty, or secure an improper advantage, or induce any act that would assist the company in obtaining or retaining business.

The Act applies to foreign agents of US companies who are located outside of the   12.06
United States, but does not apply to foreign officials who solicit or receive such bribes, ie it applies exclusively to payers.

The term 'corruptly' is not defined in the Act, although the legislative history   12.07
states that it refers to an intent to 'induce the recipient to misuse his official position'.[2] It goes on to state that the word 'corruptly' is used in order to make clear that the offer, payment, promise, or gift must be intended to induce the recipient to misuse his official position in order to wrongfully direct business to the payor or his client, or to obtain preferential legislative treatment or a favourable regulation. The word 'corruptly' connotes an evil motive or purpose and an intent to wrongfully influence the recipient.

C. OECD CONVENTION

1. Overview

The OECD Convention on Combating Bribery of Foreign Public Officials in   12.08
International Business Transactions entered into force on 15 February 1999, since

---

[2] Sen Rep No 114, 95th Cong, 1st Sess 1, reprinted in 1977 US Code Congressional & Administrative News 4098, 4108.

which time all 38 participating countries have introduced legislation in an attempt to implement it. It should be noted that 2010 is the first year that official data on enforcement efforts by parties to the Anti-Bribery Convention are publicly available, and practitioners are urged to consider that data, which was published on 15 June 2010.[3] There is a continuing monitoring process, in which the OECD Working Group on Bribery checks both the introduction of implementing legislation and its effective enforcement. Monitoring has reached phase 3,[4] with a schedule of evaluations from 2009 to 2014 in place. In addition, a Recommendation for Further Combating Bribery of Foreign Public Officials in International Business Transactions was released on 9 December 2009, when the OECD marked the tenth anniversary of the entry into force of the Convention. This Recommendation was adopted by the OECD in order to enhance the ability of the 38 states parties to the Convention to prevent, detect, and investigate allegations of foreign bribery, and includes the Good Practice Guidance on Internal Controls, Ethics and Compliance. The OECD's latest annual report is now available at <http://www.oecd.org/dataoecd/23/20/45460981.pdf>.

2. Core Obligations

12.09   In summary, the Convention obliges participating states to introduce domestic legislation that makes it a criminal offence to bribe foreign public officials in international business transactions. The core obligation under the Convention is as follows:

1. Each party shall take such measures as may be necessary to establish that it is a criminal offence under its law for any person intentionally to offer, promise or give any undue pecuniary or other advantage, whether directly or through intermediaries, to a foreign public official, for that official or for a third party, in order that the official act or refrain from acting in relation to the performance of official duties, in order to obtain or retain business or other improper advantage in the conduct of international business.

2. Each party shall take any measures necessary to establish that complicity in, including incitement, aiding and abetting, or authorisation of an act of bribery of a foreign public official shall be a criminal offence. Attempt and conspiracy to bribe a foreign public official shall be criminal offences to the same extent as attempt and conspiracy to bribe a public official of that party.

12.10   The OECD considers the distinguishing feature of the Convention to be that it 'deals with foreign bribery, i.e., it sanctions the natural or legal person that bribes a foreign public official in the context of international business transactions'.

---

[3] Available at <http://www.oecd.org/dataoecd/11/15/45450341.pdf>.

[4] In December 2009, the Working Group adopted a post-phase 2 assessment mechanism, to act as a permanent, four-year cycle of peer review. The first cycle of review under this mechanism, commencing in early 2010, is known as phase 3. It is more streamlined and focussed than phase 2 and concentrates on the following three pillars: progress made by parties on weaknesses identified in phase 2; issues raised by changes in domestic legislative or institutional frameworks; and enforcement efforts and results, as well as other Group-wide, cross-cutting issues.

The OECD Convention targets 'active' bribery only. Paragraph 3 of the   12.11
Commentaries on the Convention also makes it clear that 'Article 1 establishes a
standard to be met by Parties, but does not require them to utilise its precise terms
in defining the offence under their domestic laws'. Article 2 of the Convention
extends the ambit of the offence to bribery of foreign public officials committed
by legal persons: 'Each Party shall take such measures as may be necessary, in
accordance with its legal principles, to establish the liability of legal persons for the
bribery of a foreign public official'. Articles 3 to 17 are concerned with wider issues
relating to the application and enforcement of the offence and the practical implementation of the Convention.

3. 2009 Recommendation

The Recommendation for Further Combating Bribery of Foreign Public Officials in   12.12
International Business Transactions 2009 referred to above strengthens the OECD
framework for fighting foreign bribery by calling on the 38 states parties to the
Convention to, *inter alia*:

- Adopt best practices for making companies liable for foreign bribery so that they
  cannot be misused as vehicles for bribing foreign public officials and they cannot
  avoid detection, investigation, and prosecution for such bribery by using agents
  and intermediaries, including foreign subsidiaries, to bribe for them.
- Periodically review policies and approach on small facilitation payments. These
  are legal in some countries if the payment is made to a government employee to
  speed up an administrative process.
- Improve cooperation between countries for the sharing of information and
  evidence in foreign bribery investigations and prosecutions and the seizure,
  confiscation, and recovery of the proceeds of transnational bribery, through, for
  instance, improved or new agreements between the states parties for these purposes.
- Provide effective channels for public officials to report suspected foreign bribery
  internally within the public service and externally to the law enforcement authorities, and for protecting whistleblowers from retaliation.
- Work with the private sector to adopt more stringent internal controls, ethics, and
  compliance programmes and measures to prevent and detect bribery.

4. OECD Working Group on Bribery

The OECD Working Group on Bribery in International Business Transactions   12.13
('Working Group') is responsible for monitoring the implementation and enforce-
ment of the OECD Convention, the 2009 Recommendation on Further Combating
Bribery of Foreign Bribery in International Business Transactions ('2009 Anti-
Bribery Recommendation'), and related instruments. This peer-review monitoring
system is conducted in three phases and is considered by Transparency International

to be the 'gold standard' of monitoring. Made up of representatives from the 38 states parties to the Convention, the Working Group meets four times a year in Paris and publishes all its country monitoring reports online.[5]

5. UK Compliance

12.14   In order to ensure UK compliance with the OECD Convention, the UK Government inserted Part 12 into the Anti-Terrorism, Crime and Security Act 2001. The provisions came into force on 14 February 2002. Part 12 extended the laws against bribery to cases where the 'functions of the person who receives or is offered a reward have no connection with the United Kingdom and are carried out in a country or territory outside the United Kingdom'. It extended the laws against corruption to make prosecutions possible for 'acts [that] would, if done in the United Kingdom, constitute a corruption offence'. In summary:

- Section 108 renders it immaterial for the purposes of any common law offence of bribery if the functions of the person who rendered, receives or was offered a reward had no connection with the United Kingdom and were carried out in a country or territory outside the United Kingdom.
- Section 109 applies where a UK national or a body incorporated under the law of any part of the United Kingdom did anything in a country or territory outside the United Kingdom, and the act would, if done in the United Kingdom, have constituted a corruption offence (whether by virtue of the common law or by statute). In such a case the act constituted the offence concerned and proceedings for the offence might be taken in the United Kingdom.

12.15   It is noteworthy that Part 12 was intended to be a temporary measure, pending the introduction of comprehensive corruption legislation.

12.16   On 16 October 2008, the OECD Working Group published the Phase 2 bis report on the United Kingdom, evaluating certain aspects of the UK's track record of implementation of the OECD Convention that were of particular concern to the Member States of the Working Group.

12.17   The Group expressed its disappointment and serious concern with the unsatisfactory implementation of the Convention by the United Kingdom. The Working Group was particularly concerned that the United Kingdom's continued failure to address deficiencies in its laws on bribery of foreign public officials and on corporate liability for foreign bribery had hindered investigations. The Working Group reiterated its previous 2003, 2005, and 2007 recommendations that the United Kingdom enact new foreign bribery legislation at the earliest possible date. The Group also strongly regretted the uncertainty about the United Kingdom's commitment to establish an effective corporate liability regime in accordance with the Convention,

---

[5] Available at <http://www.oecd.org>.

as recommended in 2005, and urged it to adopt appropriate legislation as a matter of high priority.

The report found that the unsatisfactory treatment of certain cases since the 2005   12.18
Phase 2 report had revealed systemic deficiencies, including the uncertainty over the application of Article 5 to all stages of the investigation and prosecution of foreign bribery cases, and the hurdle created by the special Attorney General consent require-ment for foreign bribery prosecutions. The report found that these issues should be addressed and that the independence of the Serious Fraud Office (SFO) should be strengthened. The Working Group also recommended that the United Kingdom ensure that the SFO attributed a high priority to foreign bribery cases and had sufficient resources to address such cases effectively.

The Working Group did highlight some positive aspects in the United Kingdom's   12.19
fight against foreign bribery, including the allocation of significant financial resources and nationwide jurisdiction to a specialized unit of the City of London Police for foreign bribery investigations. The Group noted the United Kingdom's first convic-tion in September 2008 for foreign bribery in international business transactions, and an anti-corruption strategy to improve and strengthen the United Kingdom's law and structures to tackle foreign bribery.

Nevertheless, the Working Group considered that reforms were urgently needed   12.20
and should be dealt with as a matter of political priority. In light of the numerous issues of serious concern, the Working Group requested that the United Kingdom provide quarterly written reports on legislative progress for each Working Group meeting and indicated that it may carry out follow-up visits to the United Kingdom. The Working Group may also take further appropriate action after it considers the reports or any on-site visits. The Group stressed that failing to enact effective and comprehensive legislation undermined the credibility of the UK legal framework and potentially triggered the need for increased due diligence over UK companies by their commercial partners or multilateral development banks.

The OECD's findings do not accord with the comments of Parliamentary-   12.21
Under-Secretary Lord Bach, who, on 9 December 2009, during the second reading of the Bribery Bill 2010, informed the House of Lords that the issue at stake was not one of compliance or of the scope of the existing criminal law. The United Kingdom 'was and is fully compliant' with international obligations. The question was whether our criminal law is wholly 'fit for its purpose'.

The OECD has since welcomed the Bribery Bill (Act), which exemplifies the   12.22
'commitment being made by the UK Government to the fight against foreign bribery'.[6] In December 2009, the United Kingdom presented an oral follow-up report on the implementation of all phase 2bis recommendations, confirming that a new Bribery Act had been introduced. Comment on the Act is still awaited.

---

[6] Press Release, 'OECD Secretary-General Angel Gurría welcomed the introduction into the UK Parliament of a new Bribery Bill' (23 November 2009).

12.23   For those interested in the progress of the Convention, recourse may be had to Transparency International's report, *OECD Anti-Bribery Convention Progress Report 2009*.[7]

D. COUNCIL OF EUROPE CRIMINAL LAW CONVENTION ON CORRUPTION

1. Overview

12.24   At their 19th Conference in 1994, the European Ministers of Justice considered that corruption was a serious threat to democracy, the rule of law, and human rights. The Council of Europe was called upon to respond to that threat. The Ministers were convinced that the fight against corruption should take a multidisciplinary approach and that it was necessary to adopt appropriate legislation as soon as possible. They expressed the belief that an effective fight against corruption required increased cross-border cooperation between states, as well as between states and international institutions, through the promotion of coordinated measures at European level and beyond, which, in turn, implied involving states that were not members of the Council of Europe.[8]

12.25   In September 1994 the Committee of Ministers set up the Multidisciplinary Group on Corruption (GMC) and gave as it terms of reference to examine what measures might be suitable to be included in an international programme of action against corruption. The GMC started work in March 1995.

2. The 20 Guiding Principles

12.26   At its 101st Session on 6 November 1997, the Committee of Ministers of the Council of Europe adopted the 20 Guiding Principles in the Fight against Corruption. Firmly resolved to fight corruption by joining their countries' efforts, the Ministers agreed, *inter alia*: to ensure coordinated criminalization of national and international corruption (Principle 2); to ensure that those in charge of prevention, investigation, prosecution, and adjudication of corruption offences enjoy the independence and autonomy appropriate to their functions, are free from improper influence, and have effective means for gathering evidence, protecting the persons who help the authorities in combating corruption, and preserving the confidentiality of investigations (Principle 3); to provide appropriate measures for the seizure and deprivation of the proceeds of corruption offences (Principle 4); to prevent legal persons being used to shield corruption offences (Principle 5); to promote the specialization of persons or bodies in charge of fighting corruption and to provide

---

[7] 23 June 2009, available at <http://www.transparency.org/news_room/in_focus/2009/oecd_pr_2009> (last visited 7 July 2010).

[8] Explanatory Notes to the Convention.

them with appropriate means and training to perform their tasks (Principle 7); and to develop, to the widest extent possible, international cooperation in all areas in the fight against corruption (Principle 20).

At its 102nd Session on 5 May 1998, the Committee of Ministers adopted   12.27
Resolution (98) 7 authorizing the establishment of the 'Group of States against Corruption—GRECO' in the form of a partial and enlarged agreement. The agreement establishing GRECO and containing its statute was adopted on 5 May 1998. GRECO is a body called to monitor, through a process of mutual evaluation and peer pressure, the observance of the Guiding Principles in the Fight against Corruption and the implementation of international legal instruments adopted in pursuance of the Programme of Action against Corruption. Full membership of GRECO is reserved to those who participate fully in the mutual evaluation process and accept to be evaluated. The United Kingdom has been evaluated on a number of occasions, most recently on 1 to 5 October 2007.

Work on a draft criminal law Convention began in February 1996. Between   12.28
February 1996 and November 1997, there were 10 meetings and two full readings of the draft Convention. In September 1998 the final draft of the Convention was considered and submitted to the Committee of Ministers. At its 103rd Session at ministerial level (November 1998) the Committee of Ministers adopted the Convention.

An Additional Protocol to the Criminal Law Convention on Corruption was   12.29
signed on 15 May 2003.

3. The Convention

As with the UN Convention Against Corruption, the obligations contained within   12.30
the Council of Europe's Convention can, broadly speaking, be divided into five categories, usefully summarized by Transparency International as follows:[9]

- **Criminalisation:** the Convention compels signatory states to establish as criminal offences both active *and* passive bribery of domestic and foreign officials and members of assemblies, as well as bribery of officials of international organisations. Active and passive bribery of private sector employees must also be made a criminal offence. The Convention further requires states to establish as offences trading in influence, money laundering and accounting offences connected with corruption offences. The Protocol adds to the criminal offences covered, extending the prohibition to active or passive bribery of domestic arbitrators, bribery of foreign arbitrators, and bribery of domestic or foreign jurors.
- **Money laundering:** States are required to treat concealment of the proceeds of corruption as a money laundering offence, with certain limited exceptions.
- **Provisions regarding private sector:** the Convention requires states to establish the liability of companies and to prohibit accounting practices used in order to bribe foreign public officials or

---

[9] See <http://www.transparency.org/global_priorities/international_conventions/conventions_instruments/coe_criminal_law> (last visited 7 July 2010).

to hide such bribery. Thus parties are required to prohibit the establishment of off-the-books accounts and similar practices used to conceal bribery.

- **International cooperation:** given that foreign bribery involves actors in different jurisdictions and that international financial channels are often used to carry out or hide international bribery, the Convention prescribes mutual legal assistance between countries and the exchange of information. It also makes extradition easier in relation to offences governed by the Convention and provides for seizure and confiscation of the proceeds of corruption.
- **Monitoring:** The Convention provides for monitoring by GRECO, the Group of States against Corruption, which was launched by the Council of Europe in 1999 to monitor the compliance with Council of Europe anti-corruption standards established in several instruments. Technical assistance programmes are linked to the review process.

E. EU FRAMEWORK

12.31 The EU's fight against corruption comprises five limbs, succinctly summarized by the Law Commission as follows:[10]

   (i) First Protocol of the 1995 Convention on the protection of the European Communities' financial interests: active and passive corruption involving national and community officials only; necessarily confined to acts or omissions contrary to the financial interests of the European Communities;

  (ii) Second Protocol of the 1995 Convention on the protection of the European Communities' financial interests: liability of legal persons for fraud, active corruption and money laundering;

 (iii) Convention of 1997 on the fight against corruption involving officials of the European Communities or officials of member states of the European Union: active and passive corruption involving national and community officials without need for financial interests of European Communities to be (likely to be) damaged; criminal liability of heads of businesses;

 (iv) Council Framework Decision of 2003 on combating corruption in the private sector 2003/568/JHA: active and passive corruption in the private sector; liability of legal persons for active and passive corruption in the private sector;

  (v) Council Decision 2008/852/JHA of 24 October 2008 on a contact-point network against corruption.

12.32   For further information on EU activity, the reader is referred to the EU's communication on anti-corruption policy, available at <http://europa.eu/legislation_summaries/fight_against_fraud/fight_against_corruption/l33301_en.htm> (last visited 16 June 2010).

F. COMMONWEALTH SCHEMES

12.33 In April 2006, the Commonwealth Secretary General described the Commonwealth's role in the fight against corruption as 'galvanising its members to fight corruption at large, in pushing forward its own initiatives, in providing technical assistance in the

---

[10] Law Commission Consultation Paper No 185 (31 October 2007).

form of training or legislative drafting, and in implementing UNCAC in particular',[11] noting that it has been playing that role since 1991 when the first Expert Group on Good Governance and the Fight Against Corruption was convened in Harare.

In 2000 the Commonwealth published an anti-corruption plan, which was for-   12.34
mulated by a Commonwealth Expert Group on Good Governance. The heads of government in Durban had endorsed this plan in 1999. Its main findings are reflected in its Framework for Commonwealth Principles on Promoting Good Governance and Combating Corruption.[12] This defines corruption at paragraph 4 as 'the abuse of all offices of trust for private gain'. It distinguishes between 'grand corruption', 'widespread systematic corruption', and 'petty corruption'. At paragraph 22 it addresses the criminal law. It states that 'both active and passive corruption should be made criminal offences, comprehensively covering the holders of all offices of trust'. It also states that the law should criminalize money laundering of the proceeds and provide for the seizure and forfeiture of the proceeds of corruption.

At paragraph 47 the heads of government 'reiterated their commitment to root out,   12.35
both at national and international levels, systemic corruption, including extortion and bribery, which undermine good governance, respect for human rights and economic development'. Comprehensive preventative measures, including institutionalizing transparency, accountability, and good governance, combined with effective enforcement, were described as 'the most effective means to combat corruption'. A UN Convention Against Corruption was considered to be of paramount importance.

G. UN CONVENTION AGAINST CORRUPTION

1. Overview

In its Resolution 55/61 of 4 December 2000, the General Assembly of the United   12.36
Nations recognized that an effective international legal instrument against corruption, independent of the UN Convention against Transnational Organised Crime, was desirable. As a result, it established an ad hoc committee for the negotiation of such an instrument. After almost two years of negotiations, Member States of the United Nations finally adopted an agreed text on 31 October 2003.

2. Purpose

The purpose of the UNCAC is threefold: 12.37

(1) to promote and strengthen measures to prevent and combat corruption more efficiently and effectively;

---

[11] See transcript at <http://www.thecommonwealth.org/shared_asp_files/gfsr.asp?NodeID=150500& attributename=file> (last visited 16 June 2010).
[12] See <http://www.thecommonwealth.org/shared_asp_files/uploadedfiles/%7BC628DA6C-4D83-4C5B-B6E8-FBA05F1188C6%7D_framework1.pdf> (last visited 7 July 2010).

(2) to promote, facilitate, and support international cooperation and technical assistance in the prevention of and fight against corruption, including in asset recovery;

(3) to promote integrity, accountability, and proper management of public affairs and public property.

12.38   The Convention came into force on 14 December 2005, and now boasts 140 signatories. It was signed by the United Kingdom on 9 December 2003 and ratified on 9 February 2006. UK ratification was also extended to the British Virgin Islands in 2006. On 9 January 2007, Lord Lester of Herne Hill asked Her Majesty's Government what measures had been introduced or were envisaged to comply with the obligations undertaken by the United Kingdom upon ratification of the Convention to grant specialized authorities fighting corruption the necessary independence to be able to carry out their functions effectively and without undue influence. The response, from Baroness Royall of Blaisdon, was that 'UK law became fully compliant with the United Nations Convention against Corruption when the Criminal Justice (International Co-operation) Act 1990 (Enforcement of Overseas Forfeiture Orders) Order 2005 came into force on 31 December 2005, and the Proceeds of Crime Act 2002 (External Requests and Orders) Order 2005 came into effect on 1 January 2006'.[13]

3. Five Pillars

12.39   The Convention is built upon five pillars, together designed to give effect to the Convention's core aims. They are:

(1) prevention;

(2) criminalization and law enforcement;

(3) international cooperation;

(4) asset recovery; and

(5) technical assistance and information exchange.

12.40   In the first instance, the Convention requires Member States to introduce effective policies aimed at the prevention of corruption. It devotes an entire chapter to prevention, with a variety of measures concerning both the public and the private sector. The measures range from institutional arrangements, such as the establishment of a specific anti-corruption body, to codes of conduct and policies promoting good governance, the rule of law, transparency, and accountability. Emphasis is placed upon the important role of the wider society, such as non-governmental organizations and community initiatives. The Convention requires the Member States to introduce criminal and other offences to cover a wide range of acts of corruption,

---

[13] *Hansard*, HL, col WA67 (9 January 2007).

to the extent that these are not already defined as such under domestic law. The criminalization of some acts is mandatory under the Convention, which also requires that Member States consider the establishment of additional offences. The Convention also seeks to address acts carried out in support of corruption, obstruction of justice, trading in influence, and the concealment or laundering of the proceeds of corruption. The Convention also deals with corruption in the private sector.

The Convention places great emphasis on the notion that every aspect of the anti-corruption efforts it advocates necessitates international cooperation. As such, the Convention requires specific forms of international cooperation, such as mutual legal assistance in the collection and transfer of evidence, extradition, and the tracing, freezing, seizing, and confiscating of the proceeds of corruption. The Convention also provides for mutual legal assistance in the absence of dual criminality, when such assistance does not involve coercive measures. As evidence of its commitment to finding and exploring all possible means of cooperation, the Convention provides at Article 43(2) that: 12.41

In matters of international cooperation, whenever dual criminality is considered a requirement, it shall be deemed fulfilled irrespective of whether the laws of the requested State Party place the offence within the same category of offence or denominate the offence by the same terminology as the requesting State Party, if the conduct underlying the offence for which assistance is sought is a criminal offence under the laws of both States Parties.

The Convention also makes provision for asset recovery, specifying how cooperation and assistance will be rendered, how proceeds of corruption are to be returned to a requesting state, and how the interests of other victims or legitimate owners are to be considered.   12.42

The UN agency charged with overseeing the implementation of the Convention has been working closely with the World Bank in its stolen asset recovery initiative (StAR) to devise the means to assist developing countries with poor infrastructure and low governmental capacity to trace and secure the recovery of its state assets. The Basel Institute of Governance created an International Centre for Asset Recovery, with which the United Kingdom has cooperated closely. A useful overview of developments in this area can be found in Transparency International's report, 'Combating Money Laundering and Recovering Looted Gains (June 2009).[14] Transparency International, the leading NGO in the area, has much useful information on its international and UK websites and the reader is also referred to Corruption and the Private Sector 2009[15] and Transparency International UK Corruption Law and Enforcement in the UK 2009.[16]   12.43

---

[14] Available at <http://www.transparency.org/content/download/44106/707220> (last visited 7 July 2010).

[15] Available at <http://www.transparency.org/publications/gcr/gcr_2009> (last visited 7 July 2010).

[16] Available at <http://www.transparency.org.uk/publications/101-2009-publications> (last visited 7 July 2010).

12.44   It is noteworthy that the provisions of the Convention do not all have the same level of obligation. In general, provisions can be grouped into the following three categories:

(a) mandatory provisions, which consist of obligations to legislate (either absolutely or where specified conditions have been met);

(b) measures that states parties must consider applying or endeavour to adopt;

(c) measures that are optional.

12.45   This Convention, ambitious in its reach and ambit, is very much a work in progress, and represents a common global aspiration which will doubtless take many years to achieve. It is noteworthy that in the G20's Toronto Summit Declaration of 26 to 27 June 2010, the Group recalled that corruption threatens the integrity of markets, undermines fair competition, distorts resource allocation, destroys public trust, and undermines the rule of law, and so called for the ratification and full implementation by all G20 members of the UN Convention against Corruption (UNCAC) and encouraged others to do the same. The Group undertook to fully implement the reviews in accordance with the provisions of the UNCAC and agreed to establish a Working Group to make comprehensive recommendations for consideration by leaders in Korea on how the G20 could continue to make practical and valuable contributions to international efforts to combat corruption and lead by example, in key areas that include, but are not limited to, adopting and enforcing strong and effective anti-bribery rules, fighting corruption in the public and private sectors, preventing access of corrupt persons to global financial systems, cooperation in visa denial, extradition and asset recovery, and protecting whistleblowers who stand up against corruption.

Bribery Act 2010

An Act to make provision about offences relating to bribery; and for connected purposes.

[8th April 2010]

BE IT ENACTED by the Queen's most Excellent Majesty, by and with the advice and consent of the Lords Spiritual and Temporal, and Commons, in this present Parliament assembled, and by the authority of the same, as follows:—

GENERAL BRIBERY OFFENCES

1 Offences of bribing another person

(1) A person ('P') is guilty of an offence if either of the following cases applies.

(2) Case 1 is where—

    (a) P offers, promises or gives a financial or other advantage to another person, and

    (b) P intends the advantage—

        (i) to induce a person to perform improperly a relevant function or activity, or

        (ii) to reward a person for the improper performance of such a function or activity.

(3) Case 2 is where—

    (a) P offers, promises or gives a financial or other advantage to another person, and

    (b) P knows or believes that the acceptance of the advantage would itself constitute the improper performance of a relevant function or activity.

(4) In case 1 it does not matter whether the person to whom the advantage is offered, promised or given is the same person as the person who is to perform, or has performed, the function or activity concerned.

(5) In cases 1 and 2 it does not matter whether the advantage is offered, promised or given by P directly or through a third party.

2 Offences relating to being bribed

(1) A person ('R') is guilty of an offence if any of the following cases applies.

(2) Case 3 is where R requests, agrees to receive or accepts a financial or other advantage intending that, in consequence, a relevant function or activity should be performed improperly (whether by R or another person).

(3) Case 4 is where—

    (a) R requests, agrees to receive or accepts a financial or other advantage, and

    (b) the request, agreement or acceptance itself constitutes the improper performance by R of a relevant function or activity.

(4) Case 5 is where R requests, agrees to receive or accepts a financial or other advantage as a reward for the improper performance (whether by R or another person) of a relevant function or activity.

(5) Case 6 is where, in anticipation of or in consequence of R requesting, agreeing to receive or accepting a financial or other advantage, a relevant function or activity is performed improperly—

    (a) by R, or

    (b) by another person at R's request or with R's assent or acquiescence.

(6) In cases 3 to 6 it does not matter—

    (a) whether R requests, agrees to receive or accepts (or is to request, agree to receive or accept) the advantage directly or through a third party,

    (b) whether the advantage is (or is to be) for the benefit of R or another person.

(7) In cases 4 to 6 it does not matter whether R knows or believes that the performance of the function or activity is improper.

(8) In case 6, where a person other than R is performing the function or activity, it also does not matter whether that person knows or believes that the performance of the function or activity is improper.

3 Function or activity to which bribe relates

(1) For the purposes of this Act a function or activity is a relevant function or activity if—

    (a) it falls within subsection (2), and

    (b) meets one or more of conditions A to C.

(2) The following functions and activities fall within this subsection—

    (a) any function of a public nature,

    (b) any activity connected with a business,

    (c) any activity performed in the course of a person's employment,

    (d) any activity performed by or on behalf of a body of persons (whether corporate or unincorporate).

(3) Condition A is that a person performing the function or activity is expected to perform it in good faith.

(4) Condition B is that a person performing the function or activity is expected to perform it impartially.

(5) Condition C is that a person performing the function or activity is in a position of trust by virtue of performing it.

(6) A function or activity is a relevant function or activity even if it—

    (a) has no connection with the United Kingdom, and

    (b) is performed in a country or territory outside the United Kingdom.

(7) In this section 'business' includes trade or profession.

4 Improper performance to which bribe relates

(1) For the purposes of this Act a relevant function or activity—

    (a) is performed improperly if it is performed in breach of a relevant expectation, and

    (b) is to be treated as being performed improperly if there is a failure to perform the function or activity and that failure is itself a breach of a relevant expectation.

(2) In subsection (1) 'relevant expectation'—

    (a) in relation to a function or activity which meets condition A or B, means the expectation mentioned in the condition concerned, and

(b) in relation to a function or activity which meets condition C, means any expectation as to the manner in which, or the reasons for which, the function or activity will be performed that arises from the position of trust mentioned in that condition.

(3) Anything that a person does (or omits to do) arising from or in connection with that person's past performance of a relevant function or activity is to be treated for the purposes of this Act as being done (or omitted) by that person in the performance of that function or activity.

5 Expectation test

(1) For the purposes of sections 3 and 4, the test of what is expected is a test of what a reasonable person in the United Kingdom would expect in relation to the performance of the type of function or activity concerned.

(2) In deciding what such a person would expect in relation to the performance of a function or activity where the performance is not subject to the law of any part of the United Kingdom, any local custom or practice is to be disregarded unless it is permitted or required by the written law applicable to the country or territory concerned.

(3) In subsection (2) 'written law' means law contained in—

(a) any written constitution, or provision made by or under legislation, applicable to the country or territory concerned, or

(b) any judicial decision which is so applicable and is evidenced in published written sources.

Bribery of foreign public officials

6 Bribery of foreign public officials

(1) A person ('P') who bribes a foreign public official ('F') is guilty of an offence if P's intention is to influence F in F's capacity as a foreign public official.

(2) P must also intend to obtain or retain—

(a) business, or

(b) an advantage in the conduct of business.

(3) P bribes F if, and only if—

(a) directly or through a third party, P offers, promises or gives any financial or other advantage—

(i) to F, or

(ii) to another person at F's request or with F's assent or acquiescence, and

(b) F is neither permitted nor required by the written law applicable to F to be influenced in F's capacity as a foreign public official by the offer, promise or gift.

(4) References in this section to influencing F in F's capacity as a foreign public official mean influencing F in the performance of F's functions as such an official, which includes—

(a) any omission to exercise those functions, and

(b) any use of F's position as such an official, even if not within F's authority.

(5) 'Foreign public official' means an individual who—

(a) holds a legislative, administrative or judicial position of any kind, whether appointed or elected, of a country or territory outside the United Kingdom (or any subdivision of such a country or territory),

(b) exercises a public function—

(i) for or on behalf of a country or territory outside the United Kingdom (or any subdivision of such a country or territory), or

      (ii) for any public agency or public enterprise of that country or territory (or subdivision), or

  (c) is an official or agent of a public international organisation.

(6) 'Public international organisation' means an organisation whose members are any of the following—

  (a) countries or territories,

  (b) governments of countries or territories,

  (c) other public international organisations,

  (d) a mixture of any of the above.

(7) For the purposes of subsection (3)(b), the written law applicable to F is—

  (a) where the performance of the functions of F which P intends to influence would be subject to the law of any part of the United Kingdom, the law of that part of the United Kingdom,

  (b) where paragraph (a) does not apply and F is an official or agent of a public international organisation, the applicable written rules of that organisation,

  (c) where paragraphs (a) and (b) do not apply, the law of the country or territory in relation to which F is a foreign public official so far as that law is contained in—

      (i) any written constitution, or provision made by or under legislation, applicable to the country or territory concerned, or

      (ii) any judicial decision which is so applicable and is evidenced in published written sources.

(8) For the purposes of this section, a trade or profession is a business.

Failure of commercial organisations to prevent bribery

7 Failure of commercial organisations to prevent bribery

(1) A relevant commercial organisation ('C') is guilty of an offence under this section if a person ('A') associated with C bribes another person intending—

  (a) to obtain or retain business for C, or

  (b) to obtain or retain an advantage in the conduct of business for C.

(2) But it is a defence for C to prove that C had in place adequate procedures designed to prevent persons associated with C from undertaking such conduct.

(3) For the purposes of this section, A bribes another person if, and only if, A—

  (a) is, or would be, guilty of an offence under section 1 or 6 (whether or not A has been prosecuted for such an offence), or

  (b) would be guilty of such an offence if section 12(2)(c) and (4) were omitted.

(4) See section 8 for the meaning of a person associated with C and see section 9 for a duty on the Secretary of State to publish guidance.

(5) In this section—

'partnership' means—

  (a) a partnership within the Partnership Act 1890, or

  (b) a limited partnership registered under the Limited Partnerships Act 1907,

or a firm or entity of a similar character formed under the law of a country or territory outside the United Kingdom,

'relevant commercial organisation' means—

  (a) a body which is incorporated under the law of any part of the United Kingdom and which carries on a business (whether there or elsewhere),

  (b) any other body corporate (wherever incorporated) which carries on a business, or part of a business, in any part of the United Kingdom,

(c) a partnership which is formed under the law of any part of the United Kingdom and which carries on a business (whether there or elsewhere), or

(d) any other partnership (wherever formed) which carries on a business, or part of a business, in any part of the United Kingdom, and, for the purposes of this section, a trade or profession is a business.

8 Meaning of associated person

(1) For the purposes of section 7, a person ('A') is associated with C if (disregarding any bribe under consideration) A is a person who performs services for or on behalf of C.

(2) The capacity in which A performs services for or on behalf of C does not matter.

(3) Accordingly A may (for example) be C's employee, agent or subsidiary.

(4) Whether or not A is a person who performs services for or on behalf of C is to be determined by reference to all the relevant circumstances and not merely by reference to the nature of the relationship between A and C.

(5) But if A is an employee of C, it is to be presumed unless the contrary is shown that A is a person who performs services for or on behalf of C.

9 Guidance about commercial organisations preventing bribery

(1) The Secretary of State must publish guidance about procedures that relevant commercial organisations can put in place to prevent persons associated with them from bribing as mentioned in section 7(1).

(2) The Secretary of State may, from time to time, publish revisions to guidance under this section or revised guidance.

(3) The Secretary of State must consult the Scottish Ministers before publishing anything under this section.

(4) Publication under this section is to be in such manner as the Secretary of State considers appropriate.

(5) Expressions used in this section have the same meaning as in section 7.

Prosecution and penalties

10 Consent to prosecution

(1) No proceedings for an offence under this Act may be instituted in England and Wales except by or with the consent of—

(a) the Director of Public Prosecutions,

(b) the Director of the Serious Fraud Office, or

(c) the Director of Revenue and Customs Prosecutions.

(2) No proceedings for an offence under this Act may be instituted in Northern Ireland except by or with the consent of—

(a) the Director of Public Prosecutions for Northern Ireland, or

(b) the Director of the Serious Fraud Office.

(3) No proceedings for an offence under this Act may be instituted in England and Wales or Northern Ireland by a person—

(a) who is acting—

(i) under the direction or instruction of the Director of Public Prosecutions, the Director of the Serious Fraud Office or the Director of Revenue and Customs Prosecutions, or

(ii) on behalf of such a Director, or

(b) to whom such a function has been assigned by such a Director, except with the consent of the Director concerned to the institution of the proceedings.

(4) The Director of Public Prosecutions, the Director of the Serious Fraud Office and the Director of Revenue and Customs Prosecutions must exercise personally any function under subsection (1), (2) or (3) of giving consent.

(5) The only exception is if—

    (a) the Director concerned is unavailable, and

    (b) there is another person who is designated in writing by the Director acting personally as the person who is authorised to exercise any such function when the Director is unavailable.

(6) In that case, the other person may exercise the function but must do so personally.

(7) Subsections (4) to (6) apply instead of any other provisions which would otherwise have enabled any function of the Director of Public Prosecutions, the Director of the Serious Fraud Office or the Director of Revenue and Customs Prosecutions under subsection (1), (2) or (3) of giving consent to be exercised by a person other than the Director concerned.

(8) No proceedings for an offence under this Act may be instituted in Northern Ireland by virtue of section 36 of the Justice (Northern Ireland) Act 2002 (delegation of the functions of the Director of Public Prosecutions for Northern Ireland to persons other than the Deputy Director) except with the consent of the Director of Public Prosecutions for Northern Ireland to the institution of the proceedings.

(9) The Director of Public Prosecutions for Northern Ireland must exercise personally any function under subsection (2) or (8) of giving consent unless the function is exercised personally by the Deputy Director of Public Prosecutions for Northern Ireland by virtue of section 30(4) or (7) of the Act of 2002 (powers of Deputy Director to exercise functions of Director).

(10) Subsection (9) applies instead of section 36 of the Act of 2002 in relation to the functions of the Director of Public Prosecutions for Northern Ireland and the Deputy Director of Public Prosecutions for Northern Ireland under, or (as the case may be) by virtue of, subsections (2) and (8) above of giving consent.

11 Penalties

(1) An individual guilty of an offence under section 1, 2 or 6 is liable—

    (a) on summary conviction, to imprisonment for a term not exceeding 12 months, or to a fine not exceeding the statutory maximum, or to both,

    (b) on conviction on indictment, to imprisonment for a term not exceeding 10 years, or to a fine, or to both.

(2) Any other person guilty of an offence under section 1, 2 or 6 is liable—

    (a) on summary conviction, to a fine not exceeding the statutory maximum,

    (b) on conviction on indictment, to a fine.

(3) A person guilty of an offence under section 7 is liable on conviction on indictment to a fine.

(4) The reference in subsection (1)(a) to 12 months is to be read—

    (a) in its application to England and Wales in relation to an offence committed before the commencement of section 154(1) of the Criminal Justice Act 2003, and

    (b) in its application to Northern Ireland,

as a reference to 6 months.

Other provisions about offences

12 Offences under this Act: territorial application

(1) An offence is committed under section 1, 2 or 6 in England and Wales, Scotland or Northern Ireland if any act or omission which forms part of the offence takes place in that part of the United Kingdom.

(2) Subsection (3) applies if—

(a) no act or omission which forms part of an offence under section 1, 2 or 6 takes place in the United Kingdom,

(b) a person's acts or omissions done or made outside the United Kingdom would form part of such an offence if done or made in the United Kingdom, and

(c) that person has a close connection with the United Kingdom.

(3) In such a case—

(a) the acts or omissions form part of the offence referred to in subsection (2)(a), and

(b) proceedings for the offence may be taken at any place in the United Kingdom.

(4) For the purposes of subsection (2)(c) a person has a close connection with the United Kingdom if, and only if, the person was one of the following at the time the acts or omissions concerned were done or made—

(a) a British citizen,

(b) a British overseas territories citizen,

(c) a British National (Overseas),

(d) a British Overseas citizen,

(e) a person who under the British Nationality Act 1981 was a British subject,

(f) a British protected person within the meaning of that Act,

(g) an individual ordinarily resident in the United Kingdom,

(h) a body incorporated under the law of any part of the United Kingdom,

(i) a Scottish partnership.

(5) An offence is committed under section 7 irrespective of whether the acts or omissions which form part of the offence take place in the United Kingdom or elsewhere.

(6) Where no act or omission which forms part of an offence under section 7 takes place in the United Kingdom, proceedings for the offence may be taken at any place in the United Kingdom.

(7) Subsection (8) applies if, by virtue of this section, proceedings for an offence are to be taken in Scotland against a person.

(8) Such proceedings may be taken—

(a) in any sheriff court district in which the person is apprehended or in custody, or

(b) in such sheriff court district as the Lord Advocate may determine.

(9) In subsection (8) 'sheriff court district' is to be read in accordance with section 307(1) of the Criminal Procedure (Scotland) Act 1995.

13 Defence for certain bribery offences etc.

(1) It is a defence for a person charged with a relevant bribery offence to prove that the person's conduct was necessary for—

(a) the proper exercise of any function of an intelligence service, or

(b) the proper exercise of any function of the armed forces when engaged on active service.

(2) The head of each intelligence service must ensure that the service has in place arrangements designed to ensure that any conduct of a member of the service which would otherwise be a relevant bribery offence is necessary for a purpose falling within subsection (1)(a).

(3) The Defence Council must ensure that the armed forces have in place arrangements designed to ensure that any conduct of—

(a) a member of the armed forces who is engaged on active service, or

(b) a civilian subject to service discipline when working in support of any person falling within paragraph (a),

which would otherwise be a relevant bribery offence is necessary for a purpose falling within subsection (1)(b).

(4) The arrangements which are in place by virtue of subsection (2) or (3) must be arrangements which the Secretary of State considers to be satisfactory.

(5) For the purposes of this section, the circumstances in which a person's conduct is necessary for a purpose falling within subsection (1)(a) or (b) are to be treated as including any circumstances in which the person's conduct—

(a) would otherwise be an offence under section 2, and

(b) involves conduct by another person which, but for subsection (1)(a) or (b), would be an offence under section 1.

(6) In this section—

'active service' means service in—

(a) an action or operation against an enemy,

(b) an operation outside the British Islands for the protection of life or property, or

(c) the military occupation of a foreign country or territory,

'armed forces' means Her Majesty's forces (within the meaning of the Armed Forces Act 2006),

'civilian subject to service discipline' and 'enemy' have the same meaning as in the Act of 2006,

'GCHQ' has the meaning given by section 3(3) of the Intelligence Services Act 1994,

'head' means—

(a) in relation to the Security Service, the Director General of the Security Service,

(b) in relation to the Secret Intelligence Service, the Chief of the Secret Intelligence Service, and

(c) in relation to GCHQ, the Director of GCHQ,

'intelligence service' means the Security Service, the Secret Intelligence Service or GCHQ,

'relevant bribery offence' means—

(a) an offence under section 1 which would not also be an offence under section 6,

(b) an offence under section 2,

(c) an offence committed by aiding, abetting, counselling or procuring the commission of an offence falling within paragraph (a) or (b),

(d) an offence of attempting or conspiring to commit, or of inciting the commission of, an offence falling within paragraph (a) or (b), or

(e) an offence under Part 2 of the Serious Crime Act 2007 (encouraging or assisting crime) in relation to an offence falling within paragraph (a) or (b).

14 Offences under sections 1, 2 and 6 by bodies corporate etc.

(1) This section applies if an offence under section 1, 2 or 6 is committed by a body corporate or a Scottish partnership.

(2) If the offence is proved to have been committed with the consent or connivance of—

    (a) a senior officer of the body corporate or Scottish partnership, or

    (b) a person purporting to act in such a capacity,

    the senior officer or person (as well as the body corporate or partnership) is guilty of the offence and liable to be proceeded against and punished accordingly.

(3) But subsection (2) does not apply, in the case of an offence which is committed under section 1, 2 or 6 by virtue of section 12(2) to (4), to a senior officer or person purporting to act in such a capacity unless the senior officer or person has a close connection with the United Kingdom (within the meaning given by section 12(4)).

(4) In this section—

    'director', in relation to a body corporate whose affairs are managed by its members, means a member of the body corporate,

    'senior officer' means—

        (a) in relation to a body corporate, a director, manager, secretary or other similar officer of the body corporate, and

        (b) in relation to a Scottish partnership, a partner in the partnership.

15 Offences under section 7 by partnerships

(1) Proceedings for an offence under section 7 alleged to have been committed by a partnership must be brought in the name of the partnership (and not in that of any of the partners).

(2) For the purposes of such proceedings—

    (a) rules of court relating to the service of documents have effect as if the partnership were a body corporate, and

    (b) the following provisions apply as they apply in relation to a body corporate—

        (i) section 33 of the Criminal Justice Act 1925 and Schedule 3 to the Magistrates' Courts Act 1980,

        (ii) section 18 of the Criminal Justice Act (Northern Ireland) 1945 (c. 15 (N.I.)) and Schedule 4 to the Magistrates' Courts (Northern Ireland) Order 1981 (S.I. 1981/1675 (N.I.26)),

        (iii) section 70 of the Criminal Procedure (Scotland) Act 1995.

(3) A fine imposed on the partnership on its conviction for an offence under section 7 is to be paid out of the partnership assets.

(4) In this section 'partnership' has the same meaning as in section 7.

Supplementary and final provisions

16 Application to Crown

This Act applies to individuals in the public service of the Crown as it applies to other individuals.

17 Consequential provision

(1) The following common law offences are abolished—

    (a) the offences under the law of England and Wales and Northern Ireland of bribery and embracery,

    (b) the offences under the law of Scotland of bribery and accepting a bribe.

(2) Schedule 1 (which contains consequential amendments) has effect.

(3) Schedule 2 (which contains repeals and revocations) has effect.

(4) The relevant national authority may by order make such supplementary, incidental or consequential provision as the relevant national authority considers appropriate for the purposes of this Act or in consequence of this Act.

(5) The power to make an order under this section—

(a) is exercisable by statutory instrument,

(b) includes power to make transitional, transitory or saving provision,

(c) may, in particular, be exercised by amending, repealing, revoking or otherwise modifying any provision made by or under an enactment (including any Act passed in the same Session as this Act).

(6) Subject to subsection (7), a statutory instrument containing an order of the Secretary of State under this section may not be made unless a draft of the instrument has been laid before, and approved by a resolution of, each House of Parliament.

(7) A statutory instrument containing an order of the Secretary of State under this section which does not amend or repeal a provision of a public general Act or of devolved legislation is subject to annulment in pursuance of a resolution of either House of Parliament.

(8) Subject to subsection (9), a statutory instrument containing an order of the Scottish Ministers under this section may not be made unless a draft of the instrument has been laid before, and approved by a resolution of, the Scottish Parliament.

(9) A statutory instrument containing an order of the Scottish Ministers under this section which does not amend or repeal a provision of an Act of the Scottish Parliament or of a public general Act is subject to annulment in pursuance of a resolution of the Scottish Parliament.

(10) In this section—

'devolved legislation' means an Act of the Scottish Parliament, a Measure of the National Assembly for Wales or an Act of the Northern Ireland Assembly,

'enactment' includes an Act of the Scottish Parliament and Northern Ireland legislation,

'relevant national authority' means—

(a) in the case of provision which would be within the legislative competence of the Scottish Parliament if it were contained in an Act of that Parliament, the Scottish Ministers, and

(b) in any other case, the Secretary of State.

18 Extent

(1) Subject as follows, this Act extends to England and Wales, Scotland and Northern Ireland.

(2) Subject to subsections (3) to (5), any amendment, repeal or revocation made by Schedule 1 or 2 has the same extent as the provision amended, repealed or revoked.

(3) The amendment of, and repeals in, the Armed Forces Act 2006 do not extend to the Channel Islands.

(4) The amendments of the International Criminal Court Act 2001 extend to England and Wales and Northern Ireland only.

(5) Subsection (2) does not apply to the repeal in the Civil Aviation Act 1982.

19 Commencement and transitional provision etc.

(1) Subject to subsection (2), this Act comes into force on such day as the Secretary of State may by order made by statutory instrument appoint.

(2) Sections 16, 17(4) to (10) and 18, this section (other than subsections (5) to (7)) and section 20 come into force on the day on which this Act is passed.

(3) An order under subsection (1) may—

(a) appoint different days for different purposes,

(b) make such transitional, transitory or saving provision as the Secretary of State considers appropriate in connection with the coming into force of any provision of this Act.

(4) The Secretary of State must consult the Scottish Ministers before making an order under this section in connection with any provision of this Act which would be within the legislative competence of the Scottish Parliament if it were contained in an Act of that Parliament.

(5) This Act does not affect any liability, investigation, legal proceeding or penalty for or in respect of—

(a) a common law offence mentioned in subsection (1) of section 17 which is committed wholly or partly before the coming into force of that subsection in relation to such an offence, or

(b) an offence under the Public Bodies Corrupt Practices Act 1889 or the Prevention of Corruption Act 1906 committed wholly or partly before the coming into force of the repeal of the Act by Schedule 2 to this Act.

(6) For the purposes of subsection (5) an offence is partly committed before a particular time if any act or omission which forms part of the offence takes place before that time.

(7) Subsections (5) and (6) are without prejudice to section 16 of the Interpretation Act 1978 (general savings on repeal).

20 Short title

This Act may be cited as the Bribery Act 2010.

SCHEDULE 1
SECTION 17(2)

CONSEQUENTIAL AMENDMENTS

Ministry of Defence Police Act 1987 (c. 4)

1. In section 2(3)(ba) of the Ministry of Defence Police Act 1987 (jurisdiction of members of Ministry of Defence Police Force) for 'Prevention of Corruption Acts 1889 to 1916' substitute 'Bribery Act 2010'.

Criminal Justice Act 1987 (c. 38)

2. In section 2A of the Criminal Justice Act 1987 (Director of SFO's preinvestigation powers in relation to bribery and corruption: foreign officers etc.) for subsections (5) and (6) substitute—

'(5) This section applies to any conduct—

(a) which, as a result of section 3(6) of the Bribery Act 2010, constitutes an offence under section 1 or 2 of that Act under the law of England and Wales or Northern Ireland, or

(b) which constitutes an offence under section 6 of that Act under the law of England and Wales or Northern Ireland.'

International Criminal Court Act 2001 (c. 17)

3. The International Criminal Court Act 2001 is amended as follows.
4. In section 54(3) (offences in relation to the ICC: England and Wales)—
    (a) in paragraph (b) for 'or' substitute ', an offence under the Bribery Act 2010 or (as the case may be) an offence', and
    (b) in paragraph (c) after 'common law' insert 'or (as the case may be) under the Bribery Act 2010'.
5. In section 61(3)(b) (offences in relation to the ICC: Northern Ireland) after 'common law' insert 'or (as the case may be) under the Bribery Act 2010'.

International Criminal Court (Scotland) Act 2001 (asp 13)

6. In section 4(2) of the International Criminal Court (Scotland) Act 2001 (offences in relation to the ICC)—
    (a) in paragraph (b) after 'common law' insert 'or (as the case may be) under the Bribery Act 2010', and
    (b) in paragraph (c) for 'section 1 of the Prevention of Corruption Act 1906 (c.34) or at common law' substitute 'the Bribery Act 2010'.

Serious Organised Crime and Police Act 2005 (c. 15)

7. The Serious Organised Crime and Police Act 2005 is amended as follows.
8. In section 61(1) (offences in respect of which investigatory powers apply) for paragraph (h) substitute—
    '(h) any offence under the Bribery Act 2010.'
9. In section 76(3) (financial reporting orders: making) for paragraphs (d) to (f) substitute—
    '(da) an offence under any of the following provisions of the Bribery Act 2010—
        section 1 (offences of bribing another person),
        section 2 (offences relating to being bribed),
        section 6 (bribery of foreign public officials),'.
10. In section 77(3) (financial reporting orders: making in Scotland) after paragraph (b) insert—
    '(c) an offence under section 1, 2 or 6 of the Bribery Act 2010.'

Armed Forces Act 2006 (c. 52)

11. In Schedule 2 to the Armed Forces Act 2006 (which lists serious offences the possible commission of which, if suspected, must be referred to a service police force), in paragraph 12, at the end insert—
    '(aw) an offence under section 1, 2 or 6 of the Bribery Act 2010.'

Serious Crime Act 2007 (c. 27)

12. The Serious Crime Act 2007 is amended as follows.
13. (1) Section 53 of that Act (certain extra-territorial offences to be prosecuted only by, or with the consent of, the Attorney General or the Advocate General for Northern Ireland) is amended as follows.
    (2) The existing words in that section become the first subsection of the section.
    (3) After that subsection insert—
        '(2) Subsection (1) does not apply to an offence under this Part to which section 10 of the Bribery Act 2010 applies by virtue of section 54(1) and (2) below (encouraging or assisting bribery).'

14. (1) Schedule 1 to that Act (list of serious offences) is amended as follows.

(2) For paragraph 9 and the heading before it (corruption and bribery: England and Wales) substitute—

'Bribery

9 An offence under any of the following provisions of the Bribery Act 2010—

(a) section 1 (offences of bribing another person);

(b) section 2 (offences relating to being bribed);

(c) section 6 (bribery of foreign public officials).'

(3) For paragraph 25 and the heading before it (corruption and bribery: Northern Ireland) substitute—

'Bribery

25 An offence under any of the following provisions of the Bribery Act 2010—

(a) section 1 (offences of bribing another person);

(b) section 2 (offences relating to being bribed);

(c) section 6 (bribery of foreign public officials).'

SCHEDULE 2
SECTION 17(3)

REPEALS AND REVOCATIONS

Short title and chapter	Extent of repeal or revocation
Public Bodies Corrupt Practices Act 1889 (c. 69)	The whole Act.
Prevention of Corruption Act 1906 (c. 34)	The whole Act.
Prevention of Corruption Act 1916 (c. 64)	The whole Act.
Criminal Justice Act (Northern Ireland) 1945 (c. 15 (N.I.))	Section 22.
Electoral Law Act (Northern Ireland) 1962 (c. 14 (N.I.))	Section 112(3).
Increase of Fines Act (Northern Ireland) 1967 (c. 29 (N.I.))	Section 1(8)(a) and (b).
Criminal Justice (Miscellaneous Provisions) Act (Northern Ireland) 1968 (c. 28 (N.I.))	In Schedule 2, the entry in the table relating to the Prevention of Corruption Act 1906.
Local Government Act (Northern Ireland) 1972 (c. 9 (N.I.))	In Schedule 8, paragraphs 1 and 3.
Civil Aviation Act 1982 (c. 16)	Section 19(1).
Representation of the People Act 1983 (c. 2	In section 165(1), paragraph (b) and the word 'or' immediately before it.
Housing Associations Act 1985 (c. 69)	In Schedule 6, paragraph 1(2).
Criminal Justice Act 1988 (c. 33)	Section 47.
Criminal Justice (Evidence etc.) (Northern Ireland) Order 1988 (S.I. 1988/1847 (N.I.17))	Article 14.
Enterprise and New Towns (Scotland) Act 1990 (c. 35)	In Schedule 1, paragraph 2.
Scotland Act 1998 (c. 46)	Section 43.
Anti-terrorism, Crime and Security Act 2001 (c. 24)	Sections 108 to 110.

(continued)

Short title and chapter	Extent of repeal or revocation
Criminal Justice (Scotland) Act 2003 (asp 7)	Sections 68 and 69.
Government of Wales Act 2006 (c. 32)	Section 44.
Armed Forces Act 2006 (c. 52)	In Schedule 2, paragraph 12(l) and (m).
Local Government and Public Involvement in Health Act 2007 (c. 28)	Section 217(1)(a). Section 244(4). In Schedule 14, paragraph 1.
Housing and Regeneration Act 2008 (c. 17)	In Schedule 1, paragraph 16.

APPENDIX 2

Useful Links

Anti-Corruption Commission of the International Chamber of Commerce:
<http://www.iccwbo.org/policy/anticorruption/>

Anti-corruption Forum: <http://www.anticorruptionforum.org.uk/>

Attorney General's website: <http://www.attorneygeneral.gov.uk/>

BIS Corruption webpage: <http://www.bis.gov.uk/anticorruption>

City of London Police Overseas Anti-Corruption Unit:
<http://www.cityoflondon.police.uk/CityPolice/Departments/ECD/anticorruptionunit/>

Council of Europe Criminal Law Convention on Corruption:
<http://conventions.coe.int/Treaty/EN/Treaties/Html/173.htm>

Crown Prosecution Service Legal Guidance on Bribery and Corruption:
<http://www.cps.gov.uk/legal/a_to_c/bribery_and_corruption/>

EU Corruption Homepage:
<http://europa.eu/legislation_summaries/fight_against_fraud/fight_against_corruption/
index_en.htm>

Explanatory Notes to the Bribery Act 2010:
<http://www.opsi.gov.uk/acts/acts2010/en/ukpgaen_20100023_en_1>

Home Office: <http://www.homeoffice.gov.uk/>

Joint Committee on the Draft Bribery Bill Homepage:
<http://www.parliament.uk/parliamentary_committees/joint_committee_on_the_draft_bribery_
bill.cfm>

Law Commission's Bribery Homepage: <http://www.lawcom.gov.uk/bribery.htm>

Ministry of Justice Bribery Homepage:
<http://www.justice.gov.uk/publications/bribery-bill.htm>

OECD: <http://www.oecd.org/>

Serious Fraud Office Bribery and Corruption Homepage:
<http://www.sfo.gov.uk/bribery--corruption.aspx>

The Corner House Corruption Homepage:
<http://www.thecornerhouse.org.uk/subject/corruption/>

Transparency International: <http://www.transparency.org/>

Transparency International (UK): <http://www.transparency.org.uk/>

UNCAC: <http://www.unodc.org/unodc/en/treaties/CAC/index.html>

UNODC and Corruption: <http://www.unodc.org/unodc/en/corruption/index.html>

World Bank Governance and Anti-Corruption Homepage:
<http://www.worldbank.org/wbi/governance>

Index

deception 2.61
Defence Council 6.13
defences 6.01–6.20 *see also* **adequate procedures, defence of**
    armed services 2.79, 6.04–6.20
    background 2.61
    common law 2.20
    duress 2.20
    guidance 1.06
    intelligence services 2.79, 6.04–6.20
    subjectivity 1.10
definitions section
    general bribery offences 3.36–3.51
    improper performance 3.46–3.51
    relevant function or activity 3.36–3.45
delegation 8.03–8.04
Department of Justice (DOJ) (United States) 10.03, 12.02–12.03
DePuy International 9.02, 9.24, 10.04
development aid 1.13, 2.06
development of domestic law 2.12–2.54
    Anti-Terrorism, Crime and Security Act 2001 2.52
    common law 2.12–2.34
    Prevention of Corruption Act 1906 2.36–2.44
    Prevention of Corruption Act 1916 2.45–2.51
    Public Bodies Corrupt Practices Act 1889 2.25–2.35
Director of Public Prosecutions (DPP)
    Attorney General, protocol with 8.08–8.11
    confiscation and civil recovery orders 9.32
    delegation 8.03–8.04
    Northern Ireland 8.02, 8.04
    prosecution 1.24, 8.01–8.04, 8.08–8.11
directors, definition of 3.65
DPP *see* Director of Public Prosecutions (DPP)
draft bill 2.63–2.87
    adequate procedures, meaning of 2.77, 2.83, 5.23, 5.29
    agents and principals 2.65–2.66
    armed forces 2.79
    confiscation and civil recovery orders 9.30–9.31
    Consultation Paper 2.67–2.68
    fiduciary relationships 2.61
    foreign public officials 2.76, 4.37
    Hansard 2.86
    improper performance test 2.76
    intelligence services 2.79
    Joint Committee of the Draft Bribery Bill 2.75–2.79
    Joint Committee of the Draft Corruption Bill 2.64–2.65
    Law Commission 2.63, 2.69, 2.72–2.74, 2.76
    negligence 2.76, 2.82
    OECD Anti-Bribery Convention 12.21–12.22
    parliamentary privilege 2.77, 2.84
    passage of Bill 2.86–2.87
    prosecutions 2.78

public contracts, debarring companies from entering 2.77, 9.57
    reasonable person test 2.81
    Rose Committee 2.63
    Royal Assent 2.85
    sanctions 2.77
    security services 2.79
    third parties 2.65
    Transparency International-sponsored Bill 2.70
duress 2.20

economic well-being of UK 6.11
effect of problem 2.06, 2.07
employees 5.16
entry into force 1.25, 11.07–11.08, 12.08
ethical standards
    Committee on Standards in Public Life 2.57
    compliance 1.28
    prevent bribery, failure of commercial organizations to 5.04, 5.07
European Convention on Human Rights
    confiscation and civil recovery orders 9.31
    fair hearing, right to a 2.51
    financial reporting orders 9.41
    peaceful enjoyment of possessions 9.31
European Union
    five limbs 13.31
    Public Procurement Directive 1.22, 9.07, 9.54–9.61
    website 12.32
expenditure *see* promotional expenditure
expenses scandal 2.84
Expert Group on Good Governance 12.33–12.34
Explanatory Notes 1.04, 6.14, 8.03
extent section 11.05
extradition 10.10
extraterritoriality
    Anti-Terrorism, Crime and Security Act 2001 2.52–2.53
    common law 2.21
    OECD Anti-Bribery Convention 4.03, 12.10, 12.12

facilitation payments 7.01–7.09
    adequate procedures, defence of 5.28
    codes of conduct 7.06
    definition 7.05–7.06
    Foreign Corrupt Practices Act 1977 (United States) 12.02
    foreign public officials 7.02
    gratuities 7.08
    guidance 7.07–7.09
    Law Commission 7.06
    OECD Anti-Bribery Convention 7.03, 12.12
    OECD Working Group 7.03
    payer 3.20

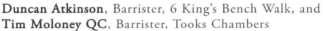

LAW FROM OXFORD

Blackstone's Guide to the Criminal Procedure Rules 2010

Second Edition

Duncan Atkinson, Barrister, 6 King's Bench Walk, and **Tim Moloney QC**, Barrister, Tooks Chambers

- Following the structure of the Rules, and including checklists of time limits and key tasks to be performed, this book is an essential purchase for criminal practitioners, magistrates, and judges

978-0-19-958870-1 | Paperback | 572 Pages | January 2011

Blackstone's Guide to the Coroners and Justice Act 2009

Jonathan Glasson, and **Julian B. Knowles,** both Barristers, Matrix Chambers

- Expert authors provide guidance on this complex piece of legislation

- Excellent quick reference tool, logically organized and following the structure of the Act

978-0-19-957958-7 | Paperback | 448 Pages | March 2010

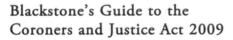

OXFORD
UNIVERSITY PRESS

Blackstone's Guide to the Proceeds of Crime Act 2002

Third Edition

Edward Rees QC, **Richard Fisher**, and **Paul Bogan**, all
Barristers, Doughty Street Chambers

• Covers the impact of the Serious Organised
Crime and Police Act 2005, amendments to the
Criminal Procedure Rules 2005, and the Fraud
Act 2006

978-0-19-953538-5 | Paperback | 576 Pages | March 2008

Blackstone's Guide to the Financial Services and Markets Act 2000

Second Edition

Edited by **Michael Blair QC**, Barrister, 3 Verulam
Buildings

• Thorough yet concise narrative exploring
how the law works in practice

• Takes into account developments in UK financial
services regulation in response to the recent global
financial upheaval

978-0-19-957633-3 | Paperback | 688 Pages | December 2009